Benchmark and Unit Tests

Grade 4

Houghton Mifflin Harcourt™

Contents

Grade 4 Benchmark and Unit Tests

Reading and Analyzing Text

Read the passage "An Art Project" before answering Numbers 1 through 6.

An Art Project

As Kasara and her brother, Darryl, strolled to school, Kasara stopped to pick up a feather, and a few minutes later, a leaf from an oak tree.

"What are you doing, Kasara?" Darryl inquired.

"I'm collecting objects to create a collage," Kasara explained.

"What's a collage?" Darryl asked.

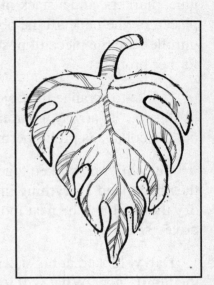

"Collage is a kind of art in which you arrange a lot of different kinds of objects and scraps on a piece of paper or cardboard, and then you glue them in place," Kasara explained. "What you get is a unique collection of colors and textures. My class has made collages a couple of times already this year."

"Other than feathers and leaves and scraps, what kinds of objects do you use?" Darryl asked.

"You can use just about anything you want. Caps of soda bottles, plastic packaging, old postage stamps, and greeting cards are some things I've used. This time, I'm also going to cut words and pictures out of old magazines and newspapers. You can even draw or paint on a collage if you want," said Kasara.

"That sounds like fun. Can I make a collage too?" Darryl asked.

"Sure. We can work on it together after we finish our homework tonight," answered Kasara.

During the rest of the walk to school, Darryl looked for objects he could use to create his collage. He continued to look for more things as he walked home that afternoon.

He found a piece of string, some shiny, colorful paper, and even some bark from a tree.

Kasara laughed as she watched him. "You're excited about this project, aren't you?" she asked.

"Yeah! I have lots of ideas about how I want my collage to look," Darryl said.

The children arrived at home and first did their homework. Then they gathered the art supplies they would need to make the collage, including scissors, glue, markers, and a stack of old magazines and newspapers. Both children placed on the table all the objects they had found during their walk. Next, Kasara unrolled a large piece of poster board and cut it in half—half for herself and half for her brother.

"I like to arrange the objects before I glue anything down," Kasara explained to Darryl. "That way, I can make changes if I want to. Once the objects are glued on, the collage is pretty permanent."

The children worked together for the rest of the evening. After a few hours, they had glued everything in place. They set the collages aside for the glue to dry thoroughly. The next morning, they each went to check on their completed projects.

Darryl looked at his sister and grinned. "You're the official art instructor of the family now. What will tomorrow's art project be?" he asked. She laughed and ruffled his hair.

Now answer Numbers 1 through 6. Base your answers on the passage "An Art Project."

1   What is the setting at the beginning of the passage?

    (A)   inside Kasara's classroom at school

    (B)   in Kasara and Darryl's backyard at home

    (C)   outside as Kasara and Darryl walk to school

    (D)   at a table inside Kasara and Darryl's house

2 Why does Kasara think Darryl is excited about making a collage?

   Ⓕ   He starts looking everywhere for objects for his collage.

   Ⓖ   He starts his collage the minute he finishes his homework.

   Ⓗ   He tells Kasara that he has lots of ideas about making a collage.

   Ⓘ   He asks Kasara if he could make a collage when she makes hers.

3 Read this sentence from the passage.

> **Next, Kasara unrolled a large piece of poster board and cut it in half—half for herself and half for her brother.**

What does the word *unrolled* mean in the sentence above?

   Ⓐ   lifted up

   Ⓑ   spread out

   Ⓒ   picked out

   Ⓓ   covered up

4 Read these sentences from the passage.

> **"That way, I can make changes if I want to. Once the objects are glued on, the collage is pretty permanent."**

What does the word *permanent* mean in the sentence above?

   Ⓕ   flexible

   Ⓖ   interesting

   Ⓗ   perfect

   Ⓘ   unchangeable

Name _____ Date _____

5 According to the passage, what does Darryl think of his sister?

   Ⓐ   She is a good teacher.

   Ⓑ   She likes to learn from others.

   Ⓒ   She most enjoys working alone.

   Ⓓ   She likes to try new things more than he does.

6 What is the theme of this passage?

   Ⓕ   Treat others with respect.

   Ⓖ   It is important to appreciate nature.

   Ⓗ   Family members can learn from one another.

   Ⓘ   Schoolwork should be completed before art projects.

Name _____ Date _____

Read the article "Uninvited Guests" before answering Numbers 7 through 11.

Uninvited Guests

Our country has been invaded! However, it's not people who are the invaders. It's plants and animals.

These plants and animals are native to other parts of the world and were brought to North America. When transplanted out of their native environments, they can damage their new homes. They cause disease, wipe out native plants and animals, and cost a lot of money to control or eliminate.

What are some of the plants and animals that are causing trouble, and how did they get here? One such plant is called kudzu, a vine that was brought to the United States from Japan in 1876.

At first, kudzu was a well-liked plant, admired for the color of its flowers. It also appeared to be useful because it could keep soil from washing away. However, the vine grows very fast—too fast. Kudzu covers land that people need for forestry and farming. It can kill trees and shrubs by uprooting them or blocking out sunlight.

Another problematic invader, this one native to Central and South America, is the giant toad. The giant toad grows to be six inches long. (That's long for a toad.) The people who brought this toad to the United States wanted it to eat certain bugs that were eating crops. Unfortunately, the toads have many babies. These toads are also very poisonous. Other animals that eat the toads can become sick or may even die.

A non-native insect that is very troublesome is the fire ant. Not only can it damage crops, it also protects other insects that hurt the crops. Fire ants have actually destroyed roads by removing the dirt from under the road bed.

When fire ants are disturbed, they swarm and bite. The ant bites hurt, itch, and burn. If the ants are swarming, it is possible for a person to be bitten hundreds of times.

Plants and animals that are not native to this environment can be pests. It can cost a lot of money to get rid of them. They can destroy crops and forests. They can also harm the plants and animals that are native to an area. It is better to think carefully before transplanting a plant or animal from its native environment to a new one.

Now answer Numbers 7 through 11. Base your answers on the article "Uninvited Guests."

7 Which pair of words from the article have almost the SAME meaning?

Ⓐ native, new

Ⓑ problematic, poisonous

Ⓒ wipe out, eliminate

Ⓓ troublesome, useful

8 What is the MAIN reason the author believes that kudzu is a pest?

Ⓕ It is not useful to people.

Ⓖ It takes over land and plants.

Ⓗ It costs a lot of money to control.

Ⓘ It makes animals sick when they eat it.

9 Why was the giant toad brought to the United States?

Ⓐ People admired its unique size and color.

Ⓑ People wanted it to eat bugs that were eating crops.

Ⓒ It had caused too much damage to native animals.

Ⓓ It had become endangered in Central and South America.

Name _____ Date _____

10 Read this sentence from the article.

A non-native insect that is very troublesome is the fire ant.

If *native* means "living naturally in a particular place," what does *non-native* mean in the sentence above?

Ⓕ not living naturally in a particular place

Ⓖ now living naturally in a particular place

Ⓗ able to live naturally in a particular place

Ⓘ having once lived naturally in a particular place

11 Which BEST describes how the author organizes ideas in the article?

Ⓐ description

Ⓑ comparison

Ⓒ cause and effect

Ⓓ chronological order

Read the passage "Sanjay's Rakhi" before answering Numbers 12 through 17.

Sanjay's Rakhi

Nina and her mother perused the marketplace, examining rows and rows of tables groaning with the weight of homemade food, jewelry, and paper cut-outs. Stopping at one table, Nina's mother held up a bracelet made of thread. "What about this rakhi for Sanjay?" she said.

Nina looked at the rakhi in her mother's hand. "It's nice," she said, "but this Raksha Bandhan, I want Sanjay's rakhi to be special. I'm going to keep looking." Nina turned back to the display of rakhis.

Tomorrow was Raksha Bandhan. This festival was always held on a full moon in August. Raksha Bandhan was a holiday just for siblings. On this day, brothers and sisters declared their affection and devotion for each other with words, rituals, and small gifts. Sisters wished their brothers well. Brothers promised to protect their sisters from harm.

Nina had always loved celebrating Raksha Bandhan with her brother Sanjay. Each year they would look forward to the holiday, the special dishes, and the presents. But this year the festival meant more to her than it had in the past.

Sanjay was walking home from school one day that spring when he saw Nina surrounded by a group of older students. At first, he was glad that she had made some new friends. But when he approached them, he saw that one of the boys held Nina's schoolbooks. Papers and pencils were scattered on the ground, and Nina was crouching on the ground, crying.

Sanjay pushed the boys aside and knelt down beside Nina. "Come on, let's go home," he said gently. He helped her gather her things, and with a scathing glance at the bullies, he led her away. No one from school had teased his little sister since then.

Raksha Bandhan was a time for honoring the bond between brothers and sisters, but until now, Nina had treated it like any other fun holiday. Since Sanjay had stood up for her, she understood what it meant to him to promise his protection. The festival now held more significance for Nina than ever. She had decided to buy Sanjay the most beautiful rakhi she could afford.

Nina wandered over to another table and looked at the rakhis. Right away one caught her eye. This rakhi had a band made of brightly colored thread, and in the center was a sunburst of gold paper and turquoise beads. It would be impossible

Name _____ Date _____

to find a rahki more perfect for Sanjay. When the salesman told her how much the rakhi cost, she grinned.

"Mom, I found it!" Nina cried. "Look what I'm going to give Sanjay!"

Now answer Numbers 12 through 17. Base your answers on the passage "Sanjay's Rakhi."

12 Where does MOST of the passage take place?

    Ⓕ the market

    Ⓖ the festival

    Ⓗ Nina and Sanjay's house

    Ⓘ Nina and Sanjay's school

13 What does the flashback in the passage explain?

    Ⓐ why the older boys teased Nina

    Ⓑ why this year's festival means so much to Nina

    Ⓒ the history behind the festival of Raksha Bandham

    Ⓓ the various ways people celebrate Raksha Bandham

14 Read this sentence from the passage.

    It would be impossible to find a rakhi more perfect for Sanjay.

If *possible* means "able to be done," what does *impossible* mean?

    Ⓕ not able to be done

    Ⓖ able to be done again

    Ⓗ able to be done quickly

    Ⓘ able to be done in a better way

15 Which word BEST describes Nina in this passage?

Ⓐ helpful

Ⓑ thankful

Ⓒ unsure

Ⓓ upset

16 What does Nina decide in the passage?

Ⓕ which rakhi to buy for her brother

Ⓖ why she wants to buy a special rakhi

Ⓗ what gifts she will receive at the festival

Ⓘ what dishes she will cook for the festival

17 What is the theme of this passage?

Ⓐ Preparing for a festival takes a lot of time.

Ⓑ A gift is only good if it costs a lot of money.

Ⓒ Giving gifts is as rewarding as receiving them.

Ⓓ Sometimes people need help in picking the perfect gift.

Read the article "Sandy Skyscrapers to Clay Cobras" before answering Numbers 18 through 23.

Sandy Skyscrapers to Clay Cobras

by Julie Brooks Hiller, P.G.
art by Karen Dugan

What in the world is coating your sneakers? Is *silt* stuck between the zigzags? Is *clay* caked to your laces? Is *sand* scraping your toes? *Gravel* gouging your heel? A soil scientist knows the difference between silt, clay, sand, and gravel. Do you?

It's simple, if you remember it's only a matter of size.

Sand and gravel are made of different-sized pieces of rock. Gravel is made up of coarser rock about the size of a marble or larger. Sand is tiny, fine, and gritty, about the size of a freckle—perfect for building sandy skyscrapers at the shore!

Silt and clay are also made of rock, but the pieces are so tiny that you can't see them with the naked eye. So how can you tell the difference without a microscope? Your fingers can figure it out. Soil with lots of silt in it feels creamy, like buttery icing. Soil with lots of clay in it feels sticky and rolls between your fingers like modeling clay—perfect for creating clay cobras!

Most folks have a mixture of gravel, sand, clay, and silt in their backyards. What's in yours? If you live on a beach, you may have only one type of soil—sand. If you live inland, perhaps you'll find all four types. Wherever you live, if you enjoy getting messy, you'll have fun performing this experiment to find out. It's as easy as pie—*mud* pie.

What You'll Need:

    1-quart bucket or bowl

    hand shovel

    1 cup water

    finely meshed wire sieve

    1 gallon water for washing

    playclothes

What to Do:

1. Use the hand shovel to dig a soil sample from the yard. (Ask an adult where you may dig.)

2. Fill the bucket or bowl half full with soil.

3. Add 1/2 cup water and mix with your hands until the thick mud sticks together like a giant meatball. Add more water if the soil is still too dry. Be careful not to add too much water. It will make the soil soupy.

4. Rub your fingers together and feel the soil texture. Do you feel rock pieces about as big as marbles? If so, you have gravel in your soil. Does it feel gritty, like sandpaper? If so, you have sand in your soil. Does it coat your skin and feel creamy, like buttery icing? If so, you have silt in your soil. Does it feel sticky, and can you roll it into a snake shape? If so, you have clay in your soil.

5. To better see the sand and gravel, put the soil into the sieve and rinse the silt and clay away with water until only rock pieces are left. What colors do you see? Are the pieces rounded or angular?

6. Congratulations! You've just completed tests done by real soil scientists, and you've discovered what kinds of soil are in your own backyard! (Don't forget to wash up before going into your house!)

Now answer Numbers 18 through 23. Base your answers on the article "Sandy Skyscrapers to Clay Cobras."

18 Read this sentence from the article.

> **Silt and clay are also made of rock, but the pieces are so tiny that you can't see them with the naked eye.**

What does the phrase *with the naked eye* mean in the sentence above?

F   using only one eye

G   using touch and sight

H   using scientific knowledge

I   using both eyes without help

19 Read this sentence from the article.

> **Use the hand shovel to dig a soil sample from the yard.**

What does the word *sample* mean in the sentence above?

A   a test

B   a piece of land

C   a large collection

D   a small part of a whole

20 What reason does the author give for not adding too much water to the soil?

F   It will make the soil gritty.

G   It will make the soil soupy.

H   It will make the soil stick together.

I   It will make the soil hard to roll into a snake shape.

21 How can the reader tell if there is gravel in the soil?

Ⓐ The soil feels sticky.

Ⓑ The soil coats your skin.

Ⓒ The soil feels like sandpaper.

Ⓓ The soil contains rock pieces.

22 Read the dictionary entry below.

sieve /siv/ *noun* **1.** A utensil, usually made of wire mesh, used for straining or sifting. **2.** a person who cannot keep a secret. *verb* **3.** to put or force through a sieve; sift. **4.** to separate or remove materials by use of a sieve.

Read this sentence from the article.

To better see the sand and gravel, put the soil into the sieve and rinse the silt and clay away with water until only rock pieces are left.

Which meaning BEST fits the way the word *sieve* is used in the sentence above?

Ⓕ meaning 1

Ⓖ meaning 2

Ⓗ meaning 3

Ⓘ meaning 4

23 How do the illustrations support the reader's understanding of the article?

Ⓐ They show different types of soil.

Ⓑ They show the steps of an experiment.

Ⓒ They demonstrate the importance of soil.

Ⓓ They demonstrate how to use a microscope.

Read the passage "Jeff's Journal" before answering Numbers 24 through 29.

Jeff's Journal

September 2

When I grow up, I want to be a chef. My friends think I am crazy; they say cooking is for girls. I don't care what they say. I watch cooking shows on television, and many of the stars on those shows are men.

I've already learned a lot about what it takes to be a chef. The library had some books about cooking. One book said that, in French, the word *chef* means "boss" or "chief." One day, I will be the Zeus of a kitchen. But instead of my cooks bringing *me* ambrosia, I will create it myself!

Another book explained all about the different jobs for the people who prepare food. A restaurant kitchen is a busy place! Millions of things are happening at the same time. Prep cooks clean the food, slice fruits and vegetables, and chop other ingredients. Pastry specialists prepare dough for baked goods and arrange fancy desserts just before they are served. Cooks on the "hot line" prepare fish and meat entrees that are served hot to waiting customers.

Apparently, becoming a lead chef is not easy. You must go to school and practice for years. In college, I plan to study the culinary arts and learn about becoming a chef. They teach you how to prepare food, cook different dishes, and make food appear attractive when it is served. When I finish college, I would like to study more in another country. Right now, my first choice is Italy because I want to learn all I can about pasta, but I might change my mind when I get older.

Both my mom and dad love to cook, and they let me help them shop, plan meals, and even do some of the cooking. Maybe that's why my goal is to be a chef when I grow up.

Name _____ Date _____

Now answer Numbers 24 through 29. Base your answers on the passage "Jeff's Journal."

24 Read these sentences from the passage.

> **One day I will be the Zeus of a kitchen. But instead of my cooks bringing _me_ ambrosia, I will create it myself!**

Why does Jeff compare himself to Zeus?

- Ⓕ to show that he wants to make food
- Ⓖ to show that he wants to run the kitchen
- Ⓗ to show that he wants to prepare food but not cook it
- Ⓘ to show that he wants to run the kitchen and make food

25 Read this sentence from the passage.

> **Millions of things are happening at the same time.**

Why does the author use the phrase _millions of things_ in the sentence above?

- Ⓐ to stress the large size of a restaurant kitchen
- Ⓑ to emphasize how much goes on in a kitchen at once
- Ⓒ to indicate how serious Jeff is about reaching his goal
- Ⓓ to show how much fun it is to work in a restaurant kitchen

26 Read this sentence from the passage.

> **They teach you how to prepare food, cook different dishes, and make food appear attractive when it is served.**

What does the word _dishes_ mean in the sentence above?

- Ⓕ plates
- Ⓖ meals
- Ⓗ gossips
- Ⓘ gives out

27 Why does Jeff want to study in another country?

Ⓐ to become a lead chef

Ⓑ to enjoy himself after college

Ⓒ to move farther away from his parents

Ⓓ to learn more about the cooking in that country

28 What does Jeff think about at the end of the passage?

Ⓕ what he plans to study in college

Ⓖ what it will be like to be a boss one day

Ⓗ how his parents taught him to love cooking

Ⓘ the experience of watching cooking shows on television

29 Based on the passage, which word BEST describes Jeff?

Ⓐ bossy

Ⓑ dedicated

Ⓒ funny

Ⓓ unsure

Name _____ Date _____

Read the article "The American Flag" before answering Numbers 30 through 35.

The American Flag

An Early American Flag

Before the end of the war for independence from Britain, Americans had many different flags. Then the first unofficial American flag appeared. This American flag had the British flag in the upper left-hand corner. The rest of the flag was covered with red and white stripes.

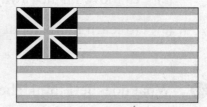

The First Official Flag

When America won its freedom, Americans wanted a new flag. They did not want a flag that looked like Britain's. American leaders met to talk about what the new flag should look like.

On June 14, 1777, Congress passed the first flag resolution[1]. It said that the American flag would have thirteen red and white stripes and that there would be thirteen white stars against a blue background.

No one knows for sure who came up with the idea for how the first American flag should look. Francis Hopkinson, who helped develop government seals, may have helped. Credit sometimes also goes to Betsy Ross, who some believe sewed the first American flag.

After the war, each star and each stripe represented the thirteen colonies. It was decided that the number of stars would change each time a new state joined the union, but the number of stripes would stay the same.

Flag Code Rules

In 1923, leaders met in Washington, D.C., to create a set of rules for how to handle the American flag. In 1942, these rules became official. They are known as the Flag Code.

[1] **resolution:** a group decision

Here are a few of the rules:

- The flag should be raised quickly, but lowered slowly.
- The flag should not be flown in bad weather, unless it is an all-weather flag.
- The flag should never touch the ground.
- The flag should be flown at night only if it is well lighted.

Today's Flag

The flag we have now dates from July 4, 1960, when Hawaii became a state. That increased the number of stars on the flag to 50. Our American flag has a rich history. We can be proud of the Stars and Stripes.

Read about other important events related to the flag throughout history.

Flag Events in History

1777	Continental Congress adopts the following: *that the flag of the United States be thirteen stripes, alternate red and white; that the union be thirteen stars, white in a blue field, representing a new constellation.* (The stars represent the thirteen original colonies: Delaware, Pennsylvania, New Jersey, Georgia, Connecticut, Massachusetts, Maryland, South Carolina, New Hampshire, Virginia, New York, North Carolina, and Rhode Island.)
1814	Francis Scott Key writes "The Star-Spangled Banner." It officially becomes the national anthem in 1931.
1869	The first flag appears on a postage stamp.
1960	The 50th star is added to the flag as Hawaii becomes a state.
1969	The American flag is placed on the moon by Neil Armstrong.

Now answer Numbers 30 through 35. Base your answers on the article "The American Flag."

30 How does the author organize ideas in the first two paragraphs?

Ⓕ The author explains the different rules that make up the Flag Code.

Ⓖ The author compares and contrasts the present-day American and British flags.

Ⓗ The author explains the events that caused America to create its own official flag.

Ⓘ The author describes in order the events that brought the War for Independence to an end in America.

31 How does the author support the idea *No one knows for sure who came up with the idea for how the first American flag should look*?

Ⓐ The author explains why the flag's original designer cannot be known.

Ⓑ The author explains why stars and stripes were important to the flag's design.

Ⓒ The author credits several people with the possible design of the original flag.

Ⓓ The author credits leaders in Washington, D.C., with officially recognizing the flag.

32 Read this sentence from the article.

Francis Hopkinson, who helped develop government seals, may have helped.

What does the word *seals* mean in the sentence above?

Ⓕ stamps

Ⓖ to close

Ⓗ symbols

Ⓘ ocean animals

33 How did the American flag change when a new state joined the union?

Ⓐ A star was added to the flag.

Ⓑ A stripe was added to the flag.

Ⓒ The background color of the star field changed.

Ⓓ The outside dimensions of the flag increased in size.

34 How does the chart help the reader understand the 1777 flag resolution?

Ⓕ It tells how the first flag was made.

Ⓖ It tells what states were added to the union.

Ⓗ It tells which leaders signed the flag resolution.

Ⓘ It tells what Congress decided the flag would look like.

35 How do the illustrations of the flag support the reader's understanding of the article?

Ⓐ They help the reader remember the rules of the Flag Code.

Ⓑ They help the reader remember key dates in the flag's history.

Ⓒ They help the reader understand how the flag changed over time.

Ⓓ They help the reader understand why the Flag Code was created.

STOP

Revising and Editing

Read the introduction and the passage "The Dance Recital" before answering Numbers 1 through 7.

Zachary wrote this passage about a girl who overcomes her fear. Read his passage and think about the changes he should make.

The Dance Recital

(1) Cho really, really liked dancing, but she did not like performing in front of an audience. (2) She happily went to dance class every week. (3) She danced around the bushes while her parents gardened. (4) She danced around the house while doing her chores. (5) However, she usually froze when it was time for her end-of-year recital.

(6) She wanted this year's recital to be different. (7) Her dad had an idea. (8) He reminded her that she loved dancing in the garden. (9) He said she should pretend the people in the audience are flowers. (10) That way it would be just like dancing in the garden.

(11) Because Cho practiced her dance every day. (12) She knew the steps by heart. (13) If she could just stop her nerves and move her feat, her dance recital would be perfect.

(14) On the Day of the dance recital, Cho tried to remain calm and cool. (15) However, by the time she changed into her costume for the show, she was not sure she could perform. (16) She remembered what her dad had said. (17) She walked onto the stage, trying to think about flowers. (18) Then she

Name _____ Date _____

looked out to the audience. (19) Everyone in the audience were holding

a flower. (20) The flowers were all from Cho's garden. (21) She saw her

father smiling at her from behind a flower. (22) Cho smiled back at him,

and then she began to dance.

Now answer Numbers 1 through 7. Base your answers on the changes Zachary should make.

1 What change should be made in sentence 1?

Ⓐ change *really, really liked* to **loved**

Ⓑ change *did not* to **don't**

Ⓒ change *performing* to **performed**

Ⓓ change *an* to **a**

2 Which sentence could BEST be added after sentence 5?

Ⓕ She danced around her room for her stuffed animals.

Ⓖ She hoped she would be a ballerina when she grew up.

Ⓗ Cho's brother took karate lessons while she was at dance class.

Ⓘ Each year she took one look at the audience and ran off the stage.

3 What type of sentence is sentence 10?

Ⓐ command

Ⓑ exclamation

Ⓒ question

Ⓓ statement

4 What revision is needed in sentences 11 and 12?

Ⓕ Because Cho practiced her dance every day, knew the steps by heart.

Ⓖ Because Cho practiced her dance every day, she knew the steps by heart.

Ⓗ Because Cho practiced her dance every day, and she knew the steps by heart.

Ⓘ Because Cho practiced her dance every day, and therefore she knew the steps by heart.

5 What change should be made in sentence 13?

Ⓐ change *could* to **can**

Ⓑ change *stop* to **stopped**

Ⓒ change *feat* to **feet**

Ⓓ change *be* to **been**

6 What change should be made in sentence 14?

Ⓕ change *Day* to **day**

Ⓖ change the comma to a period

Ⓗ change *remain* to **remained**

Ⓘ delete *and* after **calm**

7 What change should be made in sentence 19?

Ⓐ change *Everyone* to **Anyone**

Ⓑ change *were* to **was**

Ⓒ change *holding* to **hold**

Ⓓ change the period to a question mark

Read the introduction and the passage "Super Brother" before answering Numbers 8 through 14.

Julian wrote this passage about his baby brother. Read his passage and think about the changes he should make.

Super Brother

(1) My name is Julian, but my new nickname is Super Brother.

(2) I have been an older brother for about one year. (3) I just earned my nickname this morning.

(4) I was about to take a drink of orange juice. (5) Suddenly, we herd my baby brother, Grayson, crying. (6) Mom picked him up she changed his diaper. (7) Then she gently placed him on the carpet so she could wash her hands. (8) That's when Grayson began to cry. (9) In a soothing voice, Mom whispered, It's okay, Grayson. (10) But Grayson's crying only got worse.

(11) Next, Dad tried to calm Grayson down. (12) Dad picked him up and gave him kisses on the cheek, but Grayson threw his head back and wailed. (13) My grandmother picked him up and bounced him on her knee, but it had no effect. (14) He was in a very, very bad mood!

(15) My sister, Allison, took Grayson and began to sing his favorite lullaby. (16) He squeezed his eyes shut, pursed his lips, and screamed even louder. (17) It was unbearable.

(18) Someone had to calm Grayson, but no one was having any luck.

(19) As I walked toward him, I tripped over my own feet. (20) I tried to

Name _____ Date _____

catch my balance, and both of my armes shot into the air. (21) I didn't fall,

but I guess I looked pretty silly. (22) Grayson must have thought so, too,

because he stopped crying and started to giggle. (23) His laughter was

music to our ears. (24) From now on, my family. (25) They will call me

Super Brother. (26) I sure know how to make Grayson laugh!

Now answer Numbers 8 through 14. Base your answers on the changes Julian should make.

8 Which sentence could BEST be added before sentence 4?

Ⓕ My sister's name is Allison, but her nickname is Alli.

Ⓖ I'm in fourth grade, and my sister, Allison, is in sixth grade.

Ⓗ It all started as my family was about to sit down for a nice, quiet breakfast.

Ⓘ I live in a small house with my mom, my dad, my sister, and my grandmother.

9 What change should be made in sentence 5?

Ⓐ change *we* to **they**

Ⓑ change *herd* to **heard**

Ⓒ change *crying* to **cried**

Ⓓ change the period to a question mark

10 What change should be made in sentence 6?

Ⓕ Mom picked him up, changed his diaper.

Ⓖ Mom picked him up and changed his diaper.

Ⓗ Mom picked him up, she changed his diaper.

Ⓘ Mom picked up and she changed him and his diaper.

Name _____ Date _____

11 What revision is needed in sentence 9?

Ⓐ In a soothing voice, Mom whispered, It's okay, Grayson."

Ⓑ In a soothing voice, Mom whispered, "It's okay, Grayson."

Ⓒ "In a soothing voice, Mom whispered, It's okay, Grayson."

Ⓓ "In a soothing voice, Mom whispered, "It's okay, Grayson."

12 What change should be made in sentence 14?

Ⓕ change *was* to **were**

Ⓖ delete the word *in*

Ⓗ change *very, very bad* to *horrible*

Ⓘ change the exclamation mark to a question mark

13 What revision is needed in sentences 24 and 25?

Ⓐ From now on, my family will call me Super Brother.

Ⓑ From now on, my family, they will call me super brother.

Ⓒ From now on, my family, they will call me Super Brother.

Ⓓ From now on, my family, and they will call me Super Brother.

14 What type of sentence is sentence 26?

Ⓕ command

Ⓖ exclamation

Ⓗ question

Ⓘ statement

Name _____ Date _____

Read the introduction and the article "Great Taste" before answering Numbers 15 through 20.

Katherine wrote this article about taste buds. Read her article and think about the changes she should make.

Great Taste

(1) Imagine sinking your teeth into a lemon. (2) Does your mouth pucker just thinking about it? (3) Now think about taking a bite of very, very good watermelon. (4) Can you taste the sweetness? (5) If so, thank your taste buds.

(6) Taste buds are located on your tongue, on the roof of your mouth, and at the back of your throat. (7) If you look in the mirror and stick out your tongue, you can see your taste buds. (8) Right now, you have about 10,000 taste buds. (9) As you get older, you will have fewer.

(10) Scientists know that our taste buds can detect four different tastes—sweet, sour, salty, and bitter. (11) Today, scientists is studying if your taste buds detect other tastes, such as a specific flavor in food.

(12) Your sense of smell is closely linked to your sense of taste. (13) This is why the cent of baking bread can make your mouth water. (14) If you

have ever had a stuffy nose. (15) You probably noticed that things did not

taste the same. (16) For example, peachs may taste like paper!

(17) You need both your sense of smell and sense of taste to truly

enjoy your food. (18) Without them, food would have little flavor. (19) The

next time you bite into a delicious sandwich, thank your taste buds for

making it so tasty!

_____

**Now answer Numbers 15 through 20. Base your answers on the changes
Katherine should make.**

15 What type of sentence is sentence 1?

    Ⓐ command

    Ⓑ exclamation

    Ⓒ question

    Ⓓ statement

16 What change should be made in sentence 3?

    Ⓕ change *think* to **thinks**

    Ⓖ change *bite* to **bites**

    Ⓗ insert a comma after *bite*

    Ⓘ change *very, very good* to **delicious**

17 Which sentence could BEST be added after sentence 7?

    Ⓐ Your back teeth are called molars.

    Ⓑ Pretzels and crackers are salty foods.

    Ⓒ Do you like to taste different kinds of foods?

    Ⓓ They are the tiny bumps all over your tongue.

18 What change should be made in sentence 11?

    ⓕ insert a comma after *scientists*

    ⓖ change *is* to **are**

    ⓗ change *detect* to **detects**

    ⓘ change *a* to **an**

19 What change should be made in sentence 13?

    Ⓐ change *cent* to **scent**

    Ⓑ change *baking* to **bake**

    Ⓒ change *water* to **waters**

    Ⓓ change the period to a comma

20 What revision is needed in sentences 14 and 15?

    ⓕ If you have ever had a stuffy nose and probably noticed that things did not taste the same.

    ⓖ If you have ever had a stuffy nose, you probably noticed that things did not taste the same.

    ⓗ If you have ever had a stuffy nose, if you probably noticed that things did not taste the same.

    ⓘ If you have ever had a stuffy nose so you probably noticed that things did not taste the same.

Writing to Narrate

Read the prompt and plan your response.

> Most people have done something to help a friend in need.
>
> Think about what a character might do to help a friend in need.
>
> Now write a story about a character who does something to help a friend in need.

Use this space to make your notes before you begin writing. The writing on this page will NOT be scored.

_____

_____

_____

_____

_____

_____

_____

Name _____ Date _____

Begin writing your response here. The writing on this page and the next page WILL be scored.

_____

_____

_____

_____

_____

_____

_____

_____

_____

_____

_____

_____

_____

Name _____ Date _____

_____

_____

_____

_____

_____

_____

_____

_____

_____

_____

_____

_____

_____

_____

_____

_____

_____

_____

Reading Complex Text

Read the article "Sitting for Change: The Story of the Greensboro Four." As you read, stop and answer each question. Use evidence from the article to support your answers.

Sitting for Change: The Story of the Greensboro Four

On February 1, 1960, four friends sat down at the lunch counter at a five-and-dime store in Greensboro, North Carolina. Lunch, however, was probably the last thing on the minds of Ezell Blair Jr., Franklin McCain, Joseph McNeil, and David Richmond. Like many dining areas in the South at the time, this lunch counter was reserved for whites only. At this store, there was a separate standing counter for African Americans downstairs. These four young African American men had decided to challenge this unfair policy of segregation with a non-violent form of protest. They decided to "sit in."

1. What does the word *reserved* mean as used in the passage above?

_____

_____

_____

The four friends entered the store and made a purchase. Then, they sat down at the lunch counter and ordered coffee. At first, the staff ignored them. The manager asked the young men to go to the other counter. They refused. The manager called the police. Since the young men were paying customers and their actions were peaceful, the police could not do anything. The young men remained in their seats until the store closed.

The next day, Blair, McCain, McNeil, and Richmond returned to the store. This time they were not alone. Twenty-nine of their classmates from North Carolina Agricultural and Technical College, an all-black school, joined the protest. Word of the protest quickly spread, especially after the local media learned of the story. A Greensboro newspaper printed a photograph of the four young leaders. They soon became known as the "Greensboro Four." By the fourth day, more than 300 students, both white and black, had joined the sit-in. Students crowded into the store. They filled the sidewalks outside. Inside, they took up every seat at the lunch counter. Newspapers across the country picked up the story of the sit-in. The Greensboro Four had grabbed the nation's attention. A sit-in movement had begun.

2 Describe what happens at a sit-in and its consequences.

_____

_____

_____

Inspired by the actions of the Greensboro Four, students across North Carolina began their own sit-ins. In the following weeks, the sit-in movement swept across the South. Sit-in protests occurred in Florida, South Carolina, Tennessee, and Virginia. Protesters began targeting more than just lunch counters. They started protests at "whites only" swimming pools, parks, libraries, and other public places.

Major Milestones of the Civil Rights Movement

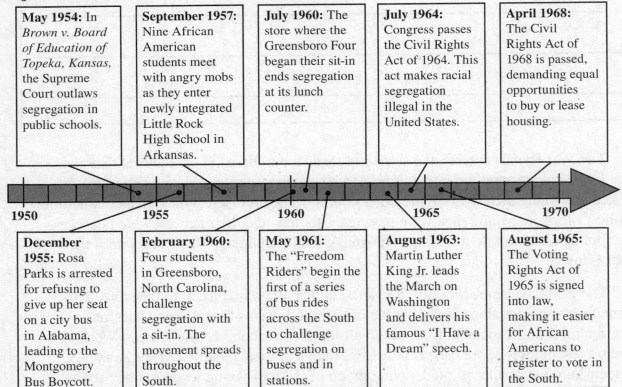

May 1954: In *Brown v. Board of Education of Topeka, Kansas,* the Supreme Court outlaws segregation in public schools.

September 1957: Nine African American students meet with angry mobs as they enter newly integrated Little Rock High School in Arkansas.

July 1960: The store where the Greensboro Four began their sit-in ends segregation at its lunch counter.

July 1964: Congress passes the Civil Rights Act of 1964. This act makes racial segregation illegal in the United States.

April 1968: The Civil Rights Act of 1968 is passed, demanding equal opportunities to buy or lease housing.

1950   1955   1960   1965   1970

December 1955: Rosa Parks is arrested for refusing to give up her seat on a city bus in Alabama, leading to the Montgomery Bus Boycott.

February 1960: Four students in Greensboro, North Carolina, challenge segregation with a sit-in. The movement spreads throughout the South.

May 1961: The "Freedom Riders" begin the first of a series of bus rides across the South to challenge segregation on buses and in stations.

August 1963: Martin Luther King Jr. leads the March on Washington and delivers his famous "I Have a Dream" speech.

August 1965: The Voting Rights Act of 1965 is signed into law, making it easier for African Americans to register to vote in the South.

3 Study the timeline on page 36. What does the timeline show about the role that the Greensboro sit-in played in the larger civil rights movement?

_____

_____

_____

In July 1960, the five-and-dime store where the Greensboro Four had bravely begun their movement finally opened its lunch counter to all customers. Four staff members became the first African Americans to be served at the store's lunch counter. Other stores in Greensboro followed suit, removing their "whites only" signs. In 1964, Congress passed a Civil Rights Act that banned segregation in public places all over the United States. By refusing to leave that lunch counter, the Greensboro Four took an important stand against segregation. Their actions helped to win a major victory for the civil rights movement.

4 Explain one major cause and one major effect of the sit-in movement started by Ezell Blair Jr., Franklin McCain, Joseph McNeil, and David Richmond.

_____

_____

_____

_____

_____

Name _____ Date _____

Reading and Analyzing Text

Read the passage "The Protector" before answering Numbers 1 through 18.

The Protector

Eagle sat high in the tree and surveyed the land below. For many years, he had protected the land, and all the animals depended on his extraordinary wisdom and strength to keep them safe. Eagle feared nothing, except for people, for he knew they were the only living creatures more powerful than he.

As the sun rose on this glorious day, Eagle was pleased because everything was as it should be. Eagle left his perch and flew around the edges of the land. As he flew, he took note of the animals. He also noticed Farmer, tending to the animals. Although Farmer took care of animals and appeared to be kindhearted, Eagle still was careful to stay far away from him. After all, the farmer was a person.

During the day Eagle kept a watchful eye on the animals. Despite the sweltering[1] temperature, Eagle remained alert all day. In the early afternoon, Deer came to Eagle and told him of a strange object she had discovered in the woods. Eagle agreed to come inspect it and followed Deer as she led the way.

Soon Deer and Eagle reached the unusual object. It was made of a shiny metal and had sharp edges. Eagle recognized it at once, explaining to Deer that it was a trap. Deer was confused, so Eagle explained that people sometimes use traps to catch animals. Eagle told Deer to leave and warn the other animals about the trap. He would decide how to get rid of it so it could not hurt any of the animals.

Eagle flew high into the sky because he did his best thinking while flying. As he was trying to figure out what to do, he noticed Mouse walking near the trap. Mouse had his head in the clouds. Eagle's response was automatic. He let out a sharp "wee-aaaa" and flew toward Mouse. Eagle struck Mouse and knocked him out of the way. The trap clamped down tightly on Eagle's leg, and he let out a piercing screech.

Farmer was working nearby and heard Eagle's cry. His animals heard the cry, too, for they became agitated. Farmer patted the animals and spoke to them soothingly. Then he went into the woods to see what had happened to Eagle.

Farmer found Eagle caught in the trap. Eagle's heart raced as he wondered if Farmer was the one who set the trap. Did this person intend to cause him harm?

[1] **sweltering:** very hot and uncomfortable

Name _____ Date _____

Farmer spoke in a velvety voice, assuring Eagle that he was there to help. Farmer freed Eagle and took the trap back to his farm, where he disposed of it. Eagle flew away from the woods and was happy that he was not harmed.

The next day, Eagle surveyed the land. He noticed Farmer working in the middle of the hot day. Farmer wiped his sweaty brow often. The next time Eagle flew by he saw that Farmer was sitting in the shade of an immense stone wall. Eagle heard a low, rumbling sound that only his keen ears could sense. Suddenly, Eagle dove towards the Farmer. He swooped down and yanked Farmer's hat from his head. Farmer stood up at once and ran after Eagle, who dropped the hat on the ground.

Farmer was confused by Eagle's actions. He wondered why Eagle would take his hat after he had treated Eagle with kindness. Just then, Farmer heard a loud noise behind him. He turned around as the old wall came tumbling down where he had been sitting just moments before. Farmer understood Eagle's selfless action and waved to Eagle in thanks.

Now answer Numbers 1 through 18. Base your answers on the passage "The Protector."

1 Read this sentence from the passage.

> **For many years, he had protected the land, and all the animals depended on his extraordinary wisdom and strength to keep them safe.**

What does the word *extraordinary* mean in the sentence above?

Ⓐ fresh

Ⓑ great

Ⓒ old

Ⓓ shy

Name _____ Date _____

2 Read this sentence from the passage.

> **Eagle feared nothing, except for people, for he knew they were the only living creatures more powerful than he.**

What is the CORRECT way to stress the syllables in the word *people*?

- Ⓕ PEO • PLE
- Ⓖ PEO • ple
- Ⓗ peo • PLE
- Ⓘ peo • ple

3 How does the setting in paragraph 1 help the reader understand Eagle's character?

- Ⓐ It shows how strong Eagle is as he soars over the treetops.
- Ⓑ It shows how Eagle tries to solve problems as he helps Deer in the forest.
- Ⓒ It shows how he watches over all of the animals from high above the earth.
- Ⓓ It shows how important Eagle thinks he is as he looks down on the other animals from the tree.

4 Read this sentence from the passage.

> **As the sun rose on this glorious day, Eagle was pleased because everything was as it should be.**

What does the word *glorious* mean in the sentence above?

- Ⓕ beautiful
- Ⓖ cold
- Ⓗ frightening
- Ⓘ usual

Name _____ Date _____

5 Read this sentence from the passage.

> **Although Farmer took care of animals and appeared to be
> kindhearted, Eagle still was careful to stay far away from him.**

What is the CORRECT way to divide the word *although* into syllables?

- Ⓐ alth • ough
- Ⓑ a • lthough
- Ⓒ alt • hough
- Ⓓ al • though

6 What can the reader tell about Eagle at the beginning of the passage?

- Ⓕ He does not trust people.
- Ⓖ He wants to trick Farmer.
- Ⓗ He has never seen a person before.
- Ⓘ He feels sorry for Farmer's animals.

7 Read this sentence from the passage.

> **Eagle agreed to come inspect it and followed Deer as she led
> the way.**

What is the CORRECT way to divide the word *inspect* into syllables?

- Ⓐ ins • pect.
- Ⓑ in • spect
- Ⓒ insp • ect
- Ⓓ i • nspect

Name _____ Date _____

8 Read this sentence from the passage.

Soon Deer and Eagle reached the unusual object.

Which word means the OPPOSITE of the word *unusual* in the sentence above?

- Ⓕ bright
- Ⓖ dangerous
- Ⓗ ordinary
- Ⓘ strange

9 Read this sentence from the passage.

He would decide how to get rid of it so it could not hurt any of the animals.

Which word has the SAME beginning syllable as the word *decide*?

- Ⓐ dealing
- Ⓑ deeply
- Ⓒ delicious
- Ⓓ dentist

10 Why does Eagle fly away from the trap?

- Ⓕ He does not want to be caught.
- Ⓖ He wants Mouse to learn a lesson.
- Ⓗ He does not want to frighten Deer.
- Ⓘ He needs to think of a way to get rid of it.

Name _____ Date _____

11 What does the author mean by the words *Mouse had his head in the clouds*?

    Ⓐ   He was trying to fly.

    Ⓑ   He was climbing a tree.

    Ⓒ   He was looking for Eagle.

    Ⓓ   He was not paying attention.

12 Read these sentences from the passage.

> **Eagle's response was automatic. He let out a sharp "wee-aaaa" and flew toward Mouse.**

What does the word *automatic* mean in the sentence above?

    Ⓕ   like a car

    Ⓖ   very brave

    Ⓗ   carefully planned

    Ⓘ   done without thinking

13 Read this sentence from the passage.

> **Eagle's heart raced as he wondered if Farmer was the one who set the trap.**

Why does the author use the word *raced* instead of the word *beat* in the sentence above?

    Ⓐ   to show that Eagle is angry at Farmer

    Ⓑ   to show that Eagle's heart is beating fast

    Ⓒ   to show that Eagle feels grateful to Farmer

    Ⓓ   to show that Eagle's heartbeat is getting weak

Name _____ Date _____

14 Which event MOST LIKELY causes Eagle to change how he feels about Farmer?

Ⓕ Farmer frees Eagle from the trap.

Ⓖ Eagle notices Farmer tending to the animals.

Ⓗ The wall falls in the place where Farmer had been sitting.

Ⓘ Eagle realizes that what Deer had found was an animal trap.

15 Read this sentence from the passage.

He swooped down and yanked Farmer's hat from his head.

What does the word *yanked* mean in the sentence above?

Ⓐ dropped

Ⓑ pulled

Ⓒ slid

Ⓓ stole

16 Why does Eagle take Farmer's hat?

Ⓕ to play a joke on Farmer

Ⓖ to let Farmer know he is angry

Ⓗ to show that he is faster than farmer

Ⓘ to make Farmer move away from the wall

17 What is the theme of this passage?

Ⓐ Kindness to others pays off.

Ⓑ You can always trust a good friend.

Ⓒ It takes courage to overcome obstacles.

Ⓓ We should work hard to protect nature.

18 Read the chart below.

Event	Conclusion
• Eagle watches over all the animals in the land. • Eagle knows the shiny object is a trap. • Eagle tells Deer to stay away from the trap.	Eagle is brave and wise.
• Farmer takes care of his animals. • Farmer speaks soothingly to his animals to calm them. • Farmer frees Eagle from the trap.	

Which sentence BEST completes the chart?

Ⓕ Farmer is lazy.

Ⓖ Farmer is kind.

Ⓗ Farmer set the trap.

Ⓘ Farmer does not like Eagle.

Read the article "Her Very Own Way: The Legacy of Artist Georgia O'Keefe" before answering Numbers 19 through 35.

Her Very Own Way:
The Legacy of Artist Georgia O'Keefe

Georgia O'Keefe is perhaps best known for her paintings of colorful flowers, animal bones in the stark New Mexico desert, and New York City skyscrapers. If you wanted to paint in the spirit of O'Keefe, however, it would not do to simply copy these images. If O'Keefe were alive today, she would surely want you to paint what you see, as you see it, in your own way. This was O'Keefe's own artistic vision. It is this vision that Georgia O'Keefe leaves behind as her legacy, like brush strokes on a canvas.

Even as a young girl growing up in Wisconsin at the turn of the century, O'Keefe was happiest with a pencil or a paintbrush in hand. She loved to make art! She was determined that when she grew up, she would be an artist. Although her parents hoped that she would become a teacher, O'Keefe enrolled in the Art Institute of Chicago in 1905. A year later, she left Chicago behind for New York City to study at the Art Students League. It wasn't long before O'Keefe began to grow discouraged with the study of art. As a child, a blank canvas had beckoned to O'Keefe like an old friend. A white page invited her to imagine all the possibilities she had to fill it. However, the students at art school were all trained in a style called realism. In this style, an artist looks at an object and then tries to copy it exactly as they see it. O'Keefe excelled at drawing and painting in this way. However, she began to doubt whether art—at least, this form of art—was her life's passion. So, for some time, O'Keefe left her studies behind.

In 1912, O'Keefe decided to sign up for a class for art teachers at the University of Virginia in Charlottesville. For O'Keefe, this must have felt like just a small step back into the art world. But this class would prove to be life changing for her. O'Keefe's teacher introduced her to the ideas of artist Arthur Wesley Dow. Dow believed that the artist's subject should be his or her own personal feelings and ideas. This idea inspired O'Keefe. This modern approach to art was unlike anything O'Keefe had ever learned. She no longer felt limited by the rules of art. She felt just the opposite; she felt free!

Armed with new ideas of what her art could be, O'Keefe moved to Texas to teach. In her free time, she painted and drew, experimenting with a style known as abstract art. She began to use lines, shapes, and colors to convey her feelings and ideas. At the time, O'Keefe was one of very few artists in the world trying out this new style. A friend of O'Keefe's gave several of her drawings to a well-known New York City photographer and gallery owner named Alfred Stieglitz. Impressed, Stieglitz put O'Keefe's work into one of his shows. He encouraged O'Keefe to move to New York to focus on her painting. She did.

Stieglitz and O'Keefe fell in love and married in 1924. A huge fan of O'Keefe's work, Stieglitz helped to promote O'Keefe's art. This was not an easy task. Until this point, the art world had been dominated by European male artists who followed traditional styles. As an American female abstract artist, O'Keefe broke completely from that mold. She challenged all traditional notions of art and artist. She painted enormous flowers, zooming in on petals and small parts. She captured city buildings and streets with abstract shapes. Her style was simple, graceful, and unique. Soon, it became well-known.

In 1929, O'Keefe traveled to northern New Mexico. She was immediately drawn to the harsh, beautiful landscapes. The mountain desert spoke to her in a way no place ever had. She wanted to paint the layers of red-gold earth, the desert flowers, and white clouds against the bright blue sky as they appeared in her mind. She began to paint part-time in New Mexico each year. After Stieglitz's death in 1943, she made New Mexico her home. From her small ranch, called Ghost Ranch, O'Keefe painted some of her most famous works. To this day, some even refer to the striking land that surrounds Ghost Ranch as "O'Keefe Country."

O'Keefe carved out a place all her own in the sun-soaked land of northern New Mexico. In the wider world of art, she had also created a place where she could paint, in her words, "what I see, as I see it, in my own way." This legacy is evident in each one of the paintings that O'Keefe has left behind for us to enjoy.

Now answer Numbers 19 through 35. Base your answers on the passage "Her Very Own Way: The Legacy of Artist Georgia O'Keefe."

19 In the author's opinion, why would copying O'Keefe's paintings not be in the spirit of O'Keefe?

Ⓐ O'Keefe did not believe one could learn art in a school.

Ⓑ O'Keefe painted in a different style each time she painted.

Ⓒ O'Keefe believed in painting what you see in your own way.

Ⓓ O'Keefe thought that you could only paint something you had seen.

20 Read this sentence from the article.

> It is this vision that Georgia O'Keefe leaves behind as her legacy, like brush strokes on a canvas.

Why does the author compare O'Keefe's legacy to brush strokes on a canvas?

Ⓕ to emphasize the mark that O'Keefe left on the world

Ⓖ to show what kind of painting style and techniques she used

Ⓗ to show that O'Keefe was careful about how she was viewed

Ⓘ to imply that only artists can really know O'Keefe's importance

21 Read this sentence from the article.

> It wasn't long before O'Keefe began to grow discouraged with the study of art.

What does the word *discouraged* mean in the sentence above?

Ⓐ bored

Ⓑ impressed

Ⓒ more hopeful

Ⓓ less enthusiastic

Name _____ Date _____

22 Read this sentence from the passage.

> **As a child, a blank canvas had beckoned to O'Keefe like an old friend.**

Why does the author compare the blank canvas to an old friend?

- Ⓕ to show that it is old and has already been painted on
- Ⓖ to imply that it is familiar and comfortable to O'Keefe
- Ⓗ to indicate that O'Keefe was growing tired of painting
- Ⓘ to show that O'Keefe had a difficult time deciding what to paint

23 Read this sentence from the article.

> **In 1912, O'Keefe decided to sign up for a class for art teachers at the University of Virginia in Charlottesville.**

What is the CORRECT way to divide the word *teachers* into syllables?

- Ⓐ te • achers
- Ⓑ teach • ers
- Ⓒ teac • hers
- Ⓓ tea • chers

24 Read this sentence from the article.

> **Dow believed that the artist's subject should be his or her own personal feelings and ideas.**

What does the word *subject* mean in the sentence above?

- Ⓕ reason or cause
- Ⓖ course of study
- Ⓗ part of a sentence
- Ⓘ main theme or topic

Name _____ Date _____

25 Which of the following is a FACT that the author uses to support the point that O'Keefe's class at the University of Virginia in Charlottesville changed her life?

Ⓐ "However, the students at art school were all trained in a style called realism."

Ⓑ "O'Keefe's teacher introduced her to the ideas of artist Arthur Wesley Dow."

Ⓒ "If O'Keefe were alive today, she would surely want you to paint what you see, as you see it, in your own way."

Ⓓ "A year later, she left Chicago behind for New York City to study at the Art Students League."

26 Read this sentence from the article.

This modern approach to art was unlike anything O'Keefe had ever learned.

What is the CORRECT way to stress the syllables in the word *modern*?

Ⓕ MOD • ERN

Ⓖ mod • ERN

Ⓗ MOD • ern

Ⓘ mod • ern

27 According to the article, what does abstract art involve?

Ⓐ drawing or painting everyday objects

Ⓑ using color and shape to show feelings

Ⓒ using lots of detail to represent a subject

Ⓓ copying something exactly as it is in real life

28 Read this sentence from the article.

> **She began to use lines, shapes, and colors to convey her feelings and ideas.**

What does the word *convey* mean in the sentence above?

- Ⓕ change
- Ⓖ communicate
- Ⓗ hide
- Ⓘ overcome

29 Read this sentence from the article.

> **A friend of O'Keefe's gave several of her drawings to a well-known New York City photographer and gallery owner named Alfred Stieglitz.**

In the word *photographer*, what does the Greek word part "photo" mean?

- Ⓐ far
- Ⓑ light
- Ⓒ self
- Ⓓ sound

30 Read this sentence from the article.

> **A huge fan of O'Keefe's work, Stieglitz helped to promote O'Keefe's art.**

What does the word *promote* mean in the sentence above?

- Ⓕ bring down
- Ⓖ make an impression on
- Ⓗ advertise or make public
- Ⓘ purchase or get a hold of

Name _____ Date _____

31 Read this sentence from the article.

> **She painted enormous flowers, zooming in on petals
> and small parts.**

Which word means the OPPOSITE of *enormous* in the sentence above?

- Ⓐ clear
- Ⓑ huge
- Ⓒ tiny
- Ⓓ warm

32 Read this sentence from the article.

> **Her style was simple, graceful, and unique.**

What is the CORRECT way to stress the syllables in the word *unique*?

- Ⓕ u • nique
- Ⓖ u • NIQUE
- Ⓗ U • NIQUE
- Ⓘ U • nique

33 Read this sentence from the article.

> **From her small ranch, called Ghost Ranch, O'Keefe painted
> some of her most famous works.**

What does the word *famous* mean in the sentence above?

- Ⓐ beautiful
- Ⓑ colorful
- Ⓒ large
- Ⓓ well-known

34 Which detail from the article BEST explains why some refer to an area in northern New Mexico as "O'Keefe Country"?

- Ⓕ "She captured city buildings and streets with abstract shapes."

- Ⓖ "The mountain desert spoke to her in a way no place ever had."

- Ⓗ "At the time, O'Keefe was one of very few artists in the world trying out this new style."

- Ⓘ "From her small ranch, called Ghost Ranch, O'Keefe painted some of her most famous works."

35 Which BEST describes the overall structure of the article?

- Ⓐ cause and effect

- Ⓑ problem/solution

- Ⓒ chronological order

- Ⓓ compare and contrast

Revising and Editing

Read the introduction and the passage "The Best Surprise" before answering Numbers 1 through 7.

Carlin wrote this passage about a time when he was surprised. Read his passage and think about the changes he should make.

The Best Surprise

(1) Last Wednesday began like any other ordinary day. (2) When my alarm clock woke me up at 6:30 A.M., I stretched and crawled out of bed. (3) My dog, Tilley, let out a houl. (4) Then she leapt up to greet me with a big lick. (5) I put on my favorite slippers and went into the kitchen to eat breakfast. (6) That's when I witnessed it. (7) There was snow on the ground!

(8) So I live in Central Texas, I do not see much snow. (9) In fact, I can only recall seeing it snow one other time. (10) You can imagine how excited I was to see real snow!

(11) Mom entered the kitchen with my younger brother. (12) She informed me that school was cancelled today because of the snow. (13) All of us eager

to go out to play, so we munched a quick breakfast and got dressed.

(14) We put on our warmest coats and hats and we took the gloves and

scarves out from the bottom of our drawers. (15) Then we moved outside

to play in the fresh snow. (16) They made snowballs, a snow person, and

a snow fort. (17) It was a really, really fun way to spend the day. (18) The

snow will be a great surprise!

_____

Now answer Numbers 1 through 7. Base your answers on the changes Carlin should make.

1 What change should be made in sentence 3?

Ⓐ change *dog* to **dogs**

Ⓑ delete the comma before *Tilley*

Ⓒ insert a period after *Tilley*

Ⓓ change *houl* to **howl**

2 Which sentence could BEST be added after sentence 7?

Ⓕ No two snowflakes are exactly alike.

Ⓖ I like winter, but my favorite season is summer.

Ⓗ It looked like someone had thrown a giant white blanket across our lawn.

Ⓘ I went to the stove and turned on the teapot to boil water for my oatmeal.

3 What change should be made in sentence 13?

Ⓐ insert **were** before *eager*

Ⓑ delete the comma after *play*

Ⓒ delete *so* before *munched*

Ⓓ change *dressed* to **dress**

4 What revision is needed in sentence 14?

Ⓓ We put on our warmest coats and hats, took the gloves and scarves out from the bottom of our drawers.

Ⓑ We put on our warmest coats and hats, and we took the gloves and scarves out from the bottom of our drawers.

Ⓔ We put on our warmest coats and hats, we took the gloves and scarves out from the bottom of our drawers.

ⓘ We put on our warmest coats and hats then we took the gloves and scarves out from the bottom of our drawers.

5 What is the BEST way to revise sentence 15?

Ⓐ change *Then* to **After**

Ⓑ change *we* to **us**

Ⓒ change *moved* to **dashed**

Ⓓ change *fresh* to **freshly**

6 What change should be made in sentence 16?

   Ⓕ change *They* to **We**

   Ⓖ delete the comma after *snowballs*

   Ⓗ delete the comma after *person*

   Ⓘ change the period to a question mark

7 What change should be made in sentence 18?

   Ⓐ change *The* to **These**

   Ⓑ change *will be* to **was**

   Ⓒ change *great* to **grate**

   Ⓓ change the exclamation mark to a question mark

Read the introduction and the article "Yellowstone National Park" before answering Numbers 8 through 14.

Juan wrote this article about a place he would like to visit. Read his article and think about the changes he should make.

Yellowstone National Park

(1) Yellowstone National Park located in parts of Wyoming, Montana, and Idaho. (2) The park was organized in 1872. (3) It was our country's first national park. (4) It was set up to protect the wilderness so that future generations could enjoy the wilderness. (5) In a national park, people cannot farm, hunt, or change the land in any way. (6) One day, I hope to visit Yellowstone to go camping, fishing, and hiking.

(7) Yellowstone is known for geysers. (8) There are more than 100 of these at Yellowstone, Old Faithful is the most famous one. (9) It goes off once every hour and a half, shooting boiling water more than 100 feet in the air! (10) That is a sight I hope to see one day.

(11) There are also hot springs at the park. (12) Underground, water is heated as it comes into contact with hot rock. (13) The heated water works its way to the surface where it formed pools of hot water. (14) The hot springs often look yellow, orange, and green because of the rocks, bacteria, and algae.

(15) Visitors to Yellowstone can also see wild animals. (16) Elk, bison, sheep, wolves, and even grizzly bears all live at the park. (17) You are

Name _____ Date _____

most likely to see it during the early morning or early evening hours when

it is the animals' feeding time. (18) When I visit Yellowstone one day, I

taking lots of pictures!

_____

Now answer Numbers 8 through 14. Base your answers on the changes Juan should make.

8 What change should be made in sentence 1?

    Ⓕ change *National Park* to **national park**

    Ⓖ insert **is** after *Park*

    Ⓗ delete the comma after Montana

    Ⓘ insert a comma before *Idaho*

9 What is the BEST way to rewrite sentence 4?

    Ⓐ Set it up to protect the wilderness so that future generations could enjoy it.

    Ⓑ It was set up to protect it so that future generations could enjoy the wilderness.

    Ⓒ It was set up to protect the wilderness so that future generations could enjoy it.

    Ⓓ It was set up, to protect the wilderness so that future generations could enjoy the wilderness.

10 Which sentence should be added after sentence 7?

    Ⓕ People can watch Old Faithful erupt on the Internet.

    Ⓖ A geyser is like a fountain that shoots hot water into the air.

    Ⓗ Millions of people visit Yellowstone National Park each year.

    Ⓘ Most of Yellowstone National Park is in the state of Wyoming.

Name _____ Date _____

11 What change should be made in sentence 8?

  Ⓐ delete the comma after *Yellowstone*

  Ⓑ insert **and** after the comma

  Ⓒ change *most* to **mostly**

  Ⓓ change *one* to **won**

12 What change should be made in sentence 13?

  Ⓕ change *works* to **work**

  Ⓖ change *its* to **it's**

  Ⓗ change *formed* to **forms**

  Ⓘ change *pools* to **pool**

13 What change should be made in sentence 17?

  Ⓐ change *likely* to **possibly**

  Ⓑ change *it* to **them**

  Ⓓ change *hours* to **ours**

  Ⓓ insert a comma after *animals'*

14 What revision is needed in sentence 18?

  Ⓕ When I visit Yellowstone one day, I take lots of pictures!

  Ⓖ When I visit Yellowstone one day, I will take lots of pictures!

  Ⓗ When I visiting Yellowstone one day, I taking lots of pictures!

  Ⓘ When I visit Yellowstone one day, I have taken lots of pictures!

Name _____ Date _____

Read the introduction and the article "Interesting Facts About Frogs and Toads" before answering Numbers 15 through 20.

Jordan wrote this article that includes fun facts she learned about frogs and toads. Read her article and think about the changes she should make.

Interesting Facts About Frogs and Toads

(1) Imagine watching the weather report on the evening news. (2) The

meteorologist predict an 80 percent chance of rain the following day.

(3) You would expect it to rain. (4) You might even get out your umbrella

to be prepaired. (5) Would you ever suspect that you might need to put on

a hard hat? (6) That's because it could potentially rain frogs! (7) No, this

isn't a scene from a fantasy movie. (8) It sounds weird but it can actually

rain frogs. (9) There have been many reports of rain containing frogs.

(10) Is you wondering how this could happen? (11) High wind or a tornado

can passed over a pond or other body of water and pick up frogs, fish, and other aquatic animals. (12) These animals will then tumble from the sky

in another location.

(13) You may have heard that frogs and toads can give you warts.

(14) Have you wondered if this is true? (15) Have no fear because it is only

a myth. (16) A human virus causes warts. (17) You cannot get them from

frogs or toads. (18) This myth may have started because a toad having

bumpy skin. (19) These bumps resemble warts, and they are there to help

conceal a toad from its enemies. (20) A frog has damp, slick skin to keep

it moist. (21) Even though you cannot get a wart from a frog or toad, you

should always wash your hands after touching one.

Now answer Numbers 15 through 20. Base your answers on the changes Jordan should make.

15 What change should be made in sentence 2?

    Ⓐ insert **has** before *predict*

    Ⓑ change *predict* to **predicts**

    Ⓒ insert a comma after *rain*

    Ⓓ change the period to a question mark

16 What change should be made in sentence 4?

    Ⓕ Change *get* to **got**

    Ⓖ Change *your* to **you're**

    Ⓗ Change *to* to **two**

    Ⓘ Change *prepaired* to **prepared**

Name _____ Date _____

17 What is the BEST way to revise sentence 8?

Ⓐ It sounds weird it can actually rain frogs.

Ⓑ It sounds weird, it can actually rain frogs.

Ⓒ It sounds weird but, it can actually rain frogs.

Ⓓ It sounds weird, but it can actually rain frogs.

18 What is the BEST way to revise sentence 10?

Ⓐ You wondering how this could happen?

Ⓑ Do you wondering how this could happen?

Ⓒ Are you wondering how this could happen?

Ⓓ Was you wondering how this could happen?

19 What change should be made in sentence 11?

Ⓕ change *or* to **and**

Ⓖ change *can* to **could**

Ⓗ change *passed* to **pass**

Ⓘ insert a comma after *water*

20 What change should be made in sentence 18?

Ⓕ change *This* to **These**

Ⓖ change *started* to **starts**

Ⓗ change *because* to **although**

Ⓘ change *having* to **has**

Name _____ Date _____

Writing to Inform

Read the prompt and plan your response.

Most people have had a problem that they had to solve.

Think about a problem you have had and the steps you took to solve it.

Now write to explain the problem you had and the steps you took to solve it.

Use this space to make your notes before you begin writing. The writing on this page will NOT be scored.

_____

_____

_____

_____

_____

_____

_____

Name _____ Date _____

Begin writing your response here. The writing on this page and the next page WILL be scored.

_____

_____

_____

_____

_____

_____

_____

_____

_____

_____

_____

_____

_____

_____

_____

Name _____ Date _____

_____

_____

_____

_____

_____

_____

_____

_____

_____

_____

_____

_____

_____

_____

_____

Reading Complex Text

Read the passage "Charlie *Who*?" As you read, stop and answer each question. Use evidence from the passage to support your answers.

"Charlie *Who*?"

Dominic glanced at the clock and groaned. At this rate, they would never make it to the movie on time! His grandpa, who loved movies as much as Dominic, had promised to take him to see the newest computer-animated 3D film that afternoon but only if Dominic had first gotten a good start on his project. Mr. Shaw, Dominic's fourth grade teacher, had assigned the class a project for Art Appreciation Week. The students were supposed to research an artist and present interesting facts about the artist to the class on Friday. Dominic was stuck on step one: choosing an artist. He sighed, closed his notebook, and wandered into the living room where his grandpa was watching what Dominic called "that old movie channel."

1 What are TWO details in the section above that show Dominic is frustrated?

_____

_____

_____

Despite their shared love of movies, Dominic never understood why Grandpa enjoyed watching old black-and-white films when he could watch movies with computer-animated action scenes, daring stunts, and other special effects. "How's that project going?" Grandpa asked, as Dominic plopped down on the couch next to him and buried his face in the pillows.

"Terrible," Dominic mumbled through the pillows. "I can't think of an artist to research." Dominic's grandpa responded with a loud burst of laughter. "Grandpa!" Dominic exclaimed. "It's not funny. We're probably going to miss that movie."

"Oh, I'm sorry, Dominic. I wasn't laughing at you. I was laughing at Charlie," Grandpa said.

Name _____ Date _____

"Charlie *who*?" Dominic asked, sitting up. On the television, a man with a funny moustache waddled back and forth across the screen. He was dressed in baggy pants, a too-small tailcoat, a too-large pair of shoes, and a top hat.

"Charlie Chaplin! He is one of the funniest, most beloved film stars of all time. Not only was he a star, he was also a writer, producer, and director. Talk about an artist!" As another man chased Charlie's character out of the scene, Grandpa chuckled.

"But Grandpa, there isn't even any talking in this movie. How can you follow the story if the characters don't talk?" Dominic asked.

"Old Charlie is a master. Just watch; no dialogue is necessary!" Skeptical, Dominic turned to the television.

---

2 Tell how Dominic's taste in movies differs from his grandpa's taste in movies.

_____

_____

_____

In the movie, a crowd gathered to watch an old-fashioned automobile race. A camera crew was filming the race, but Charlie's character kept getting in the way, trying to get in front of the camera. Dominic had to admit, the actor, with his expressive face and dramatic gestures, was pretty funny. Dominic soon found himself chuckling alongside his grandpa, rooting for Charlie's character to succeed in getting on camera.

"What else do you know about Charlie Chaplin?" Dominic asked when the film credits rolled. He leapt up from the couch and sauntered across the room with an exaggerated stride, doing his best to mimic Charlie's character, performing as if in front of a camera himself.

"Looks like you've found yourself an artist for that project!" Grandpa said. "And if we can find you a top hat, a cane, and a funny moustache," he added, nodding at Dominic's antics, "you'll have a very entertaining presentation for your class!"

Dominic's eyes lit up. "That's a great idea! Come on, Grandpa! I think the library closes in an hour. I have some research to do!"

70

Name _____ Date _____

3 What does Dominic plan to do for his presentation?

_____

_____

_____

Dominic's grandpa laughed, poking out his bottom lip. He pretended to be hurt. "What about that movie we were going to go see?"

"Maybe next weekend, Grandpa. Or, instead, we could rent a bunch of old Charlie Chaplin movies and make some popcorn."

4 Tell how Dominic's attitude about movies changes by the end of the passage. Then tell how his attitude about his school project changes.

_____

_____

_____

_____

_____

Reading and Analyzing Text

Read the article "Digging for Africa's Lost Dinosaurs" before answering Numbers 1 through 6.

Digging for Africa's Lost Dinosaurs

by Lesley Reed

"Paleontology is more than science," says world-famous paleontologist Paul Sereno. "You get to travel, meet new people, and have adventures." He should know—he's spent 15 years on one of the greatest dinosaur adventures ever.

For millions of years, dinosaur fossils have lain untouched in Africa's Sahara desert—that is, until Sereno decided to brave the extreme heat and harsh travel. Before Sereno went to Africa, very few dinosaurs had been discovered on that continent. Sereno knew that the secret to finding lots of new fossils was to go where no one else had gone. But crossing the Sahara to search for fossils was not going to be easy.

On Sereno's first expedition, he and his team crossed 1,500 miles of desert. They climbed over sand dunes the size of mountains. When they arrived in the country of Niger, the government wouldn't allow them to dig. And robbers were such a problem that the team needed an armed guard. After working everything out, they had only a short time to do their work. But they discovered a dinosaur gold mine. Sereno and his team found one of the richest dinosaur "beds" in Africa.

Paul Sereno discovering the thighbone of the *Jobaria*, a dinosaur that weighed about 20 tons.

Within days, they found the remains of a new meat-eating dinosaur. Bigger and faster than Allosaurus, they named it *Afrovenator*, for "African hunter." They found and named many others. *Suchomimus* had a sail on its back and a long crocodile-like snout used for catching fish. (The Sahara once had a lot of water.) *Nigersauras* had 600 teeth. And *Sarcosuchus* was a crocodile-like dinosaur as long as a bus.

Workers and others crowd around the skeleton of a *Suchomimus*, which may have been 36 feet long and 12 feet high.

There are many challenges to working in the Sahara. With temperatures over 120 degrees, it's easy to feel like a cookie baking in an oven. Fortunately, Sereno doesn't mind. "I adapt to heat like a lizard," he says. And he drinks lots of water.

Where does he get water in the desert? He and his team carry it with them. From medical supplies to freeze-dried ice cream bars, the team takes whatever they need. On one trip, they carried 600 pounds of pasta and 4,000 gallons of water.

All the effort is worth it. "Every dinosaur we've found in Africa is new," says Sereno. "Not one is the same as those on other continents. That's why it's thrilling— it's a lost world."

Measuring the length of a *Sarcosuchus*, the "Super Croc," which was about 40 feet long.

Name _____ Date _____

**Now answer Numbers 1 through 6. Base your answers on the article
"Digging for Africa's Lost Dinosaurs."**

1   Read this sentence from the article.

> **"Paleontology is more than science," says world-famous
> paleontologist Paul Sereno.**

What does the suffix -*ologist* in the word *paleontologist* mean?

Ⓐ   one who studies

Ⓑ   one who experiences life

Ⓒ   one who travels the world

Ⓓ   one who believes in science

2   Why were dinosaur fossils untouched in the Sahara desert for millions of years?

Ⓕ   Very few dinosaurs had lived in Africa.

Ⓖ   The heat had destroyed most of the fossils there.

Ⓗ   The harsh environment had made it difficult to dig for fossils.

Ⓘ   African governments had made it illegal to dig for fossils there.

3   Read this sentence from the article.

> **On Sereno's first expedition, he and his team crossed 1,500 miles
> of desert.**

What does the word *expedition* mean in the sentence above?

Ⓐ   course

Ⓑ   invention

Ⓒ   journey

Ⓓ   model

Name _____ Date _____

4 Read this sentence form the article.

> **But they discovered a dinosaur gold mine.**

Why does the author compare the dinosaur beds to *a gold mine* in the sentence above?

- Ⓕ The fossils they found were numerous.
- Ⓖ The fossils had been buried with treasures.
- Ⓗ The team risked being trapped inside their digs.
- Ⓘ The team had to dig very deep for what they found.

5 Which of the following facts BEST supports Sereno's opinion that fossil digs in the Sahara are worth the effort?

- Ⓐ The climate of the Sahara is ideal for fossil digs.
- Ⓑ Every dinosaur fossil Sereno's team found is new.
- Ⓒ Sereno has developed lasting relationships with his team.
- Ⓓ Sereno's team has been paid generously for their discoveries.

6 How do the photographs BEST support the ideas in the article?

- Ⓕ They show the different supplies that Sereno and his team carried.
- Ⓖ They show a variety of places in the world that Sereno has traveled and worked.
- Ⓗ They show some of the fossil discoveries that Sereno's team made in the Sahara.
- Ⓘ They show some of the challenges that Sereno's team faced working in the desert.

Name _____ Date _____

Read the passage "Being a Good Friend" before answering Numbers 7 through 12.

Being a Good Friend

Ellie hummed to herself as she waited for Jada at their usual meeting place, the oak tree by the traffic light. The two classmates had been best friends since they were introduced to each other in kindergarten. They met at that spot almost every day after school was dismissed, and then, laughing and chatting, they accompanied each other for the walk home.

Ellie's apartment building was the first stop. The girls would arrive there, have some refreshments[1], and stay for a while to play and to visit.

As Ellie waited this afternoon, she scanned the lawn for four-leaf clovers that she could give to Jada, because Jada considered them a sign of good luck.

Ellie was concentrating so hard on her search that she didn't notice Jada had passed by. When she looked up, she saw Jada walking with Katie, whose family had just moved there from out of state.

Ellie scrambled to her feet and reached for her knapsack. She called out to Jada, but her friend acted as if she had not heard. Ellie raced down the street until she caught up with Jada.

"Hey, did you forget about me?" Ellie asked.

Jada and Katie exchanged glances. Then Jada looked coolly at Ellie.

"I thought I saw you sitting there, but I wasn't sure," she said.

"Why didn't you say anything?"

"You were so busy picking at the grass, I didn't want to disturb you," Jada said.

Her new friend giggled and made no effort to hide her amusement. Ellie felt embarrassed and confused at the idea of Jada making fun of her. She turned away abruptly and walked to her house alone. After closing the door behind her, she peered out the window as the two girls walked together past her house.

The next day, Ellie wondered if Jada would call for her on her way to school. However, when she saw Jada approaching with her new friend, Ellie hid in the

[1] **refreshments:** food or drink

Name _____ Date _____

living room until they were out of sight. Later she trudged to school by herself, feeling more alone than she had ever felt in her life.

After the dismissal bell sounded, Ellie waited again by the oak tree. This time, she didn't search for clovers. Instead, she pretended to be fascinated by her math textbook. When she heard giggling, she knew that Jada and her new friend were nearby. Again, Jada did not stop to give a greeting, so Ellie continued to read as if there were nothing else in the world except that textbook. Inside, however, she felt very sad.

As the days passed, Ellie no longer waited for Jada after school by the oak tree. Ellie missed her friend, but she didn't know how to attract her attention, so she decided to just leave it alone.

One Friday, Ellie noticed Jada leaning up against the bark of the oak tree. She walked over and said hello. Jada smiled shyly.

"I've been such a bad friend," said Jada regretfully. "I'm sorry."

"It's okay," answered Ellie, though the expression on her face showed that it really wasn't.

"It was interesting to meet Katie," Jada went on. "We have a lot of the same interests, you know. But I know that was no excuse to treat you poorly. Now Katie has found a new friend, and I think I know just how you felt. Ellie, can you forgive me?"

When Ellie said yes this time, she meant it sincerely.

"I have something for you," said Jada. She displayed a four-leaf clover, which she had carefully glued to a hand-painted cardboard rectangle. Plastic wrap protected the leaves.

"I found it yesterday in my front yard," Jada went on. "I know it's good luck, since you are still my friend!"

Now answer Numbers 7 through 12. Base your answers on the passage "Being a Good Friend."

7 What is the setting at the beginning of the passage?

(A) at the bus stop

(B) in Jada's front yard

(C) in Ellie's living room

(D) on a neighborhood street

8 Why does Jada refuse to answer when Ellie calls out to her?

(F) She does not realize Ellie is there.

(G) She is with Katie and ignoring Ellie.

(H) She has been trying to hide from Ellie.

(I) She is too interested in her math textbook.

9 Read this sentence from the passage.

"I've been such a bad friend," said Jada regretfully.

What does the word *regretfully* mean in the sentence above?

(A) with a lack of awareness

(B) with great confidence in oneself

(C) with a sense of sadness or disappointment

(D) with deep anger over someone else's actions

10 Which event helps Jada realize how poorly she has treated Ellie?

(F) Ellie tells her how hurt she is.

(G) Katie treats Jada the same way.

(H) Ellie's family moves to another state.

(I) Katie tells Jada she has been mean to Ellie.

11 What does Jada give to Ellie at the END of the passage?

Ⓐ a four-leaf clover

Ⓑ her math textbook

Ⓒ a painting she has made

Ⓓ a snack they had once enjoyed together

12 What is the theme of the passage?

Ⓕ A good friend would never do anything bad to you.

Ⓖ A good friend knows when he or she is being a bad friend.

Ⓗ It is too hard for anyone to be a good friend all of the time.

Ⓘ It is best to not expect much from your friends so you don't get hurt.

Read the articles "Good Health" and "Advice for a Healthy Heart" before answering Numbers 13 through 18.

Good Health

What's so great about exercise? Even if the thought of jogging around a track, jumping rope, or getting hot and dirty makes you shudder, there are ways that working out can still be fun. You might enjoy a game like volleyball, or maybe you ride your bicycle with friends. You could also get moving through the daily responsibility of walking your dog.

These are all ways to work out, or exercise. Exercise is a must in order to gain and preserve good health. It strengthens your body, gives you more energy, and even makes you feel happier.

When you exercise, you use your muscles. This makes them stronger, including muscles deep inside the body, such as your heart. The job of the heart muscle is to pump blood throughout the body. The blood contains oxygen, which reaches every part of the body by coursing through blood vessels. A strong heart gets the job done more effectively and with less effort. It certainly is worthwhile to strengthen that muscle.

When you are healthy, you feel like you have more energy. Energy is the power to move around. A healthy body does not have to work as hard to move, and it does not get tired as quickly.

Another plus about exercise is that it makes you feel good. Exercise causes the body to produce a kind of chemical in the brain that calms you and raises your spirits too. This chemical change is in addition to the good feelings you get from being stronger and having more energy.

Eating right is another way to stay healthy. Breakfast is very important if you make it a healthy one. It provides power to your body and to your brain.

It's easier to choose healthy foods if you know what you need. Children generally need about a cup and a half of fruit and a cup and a half of vegetables every day.

The final ingredient for good health is to get enough rest. Growing children need an average of nine hours of sleep every night. When the body is asleep, it repairs itself.

The body is like a machine. If you take good care of it, it can work well for a long time.

Name _____ Date _____

Advice for a Healthy Heart

by Dr. Goodson

Every day, my patients want to know about their heart. As a doctor, I tell them that their heart, *like all muscles*, needs to be exercised to stay strong. The other muscles in their body can just stop and rest if they become tired. But not their heart! Muscles that can stop if you want them to are called voluntary muscles. The heart, however, is an involuntary muscle that must keep working. It cannot stop.

The heartbeat is the muscle working. Every time your heart beats, it sends blood throughout the body. That is how the body gets its oxygen. The blood contains oxygen. As blood is delivered to where the body needs it, the oxygen is used up. So, one side of the heart sends blood to the lungs to get more oxygen. The other side sends the blood to the body with a new supply of oxygen.

Exercise is important because it strengthens the heart. Exercise makes our body use more oxygen so that the heart has to pump more blood. It sends more blood by increasing the number of times it beats every minute and by increasing the amount of blood with each beat. When we exercise, our arm and leg muscles get bigger and stronger. Well, so does the heart! The heart is made stronger by exercise, which makes it more efficient. Thus, we feel better even when doing normal daily activities. We feel as if we have more energy. The more we exercise, the better we feel, even when doing difficult things. Think about a time when you finished a good workout. Did you feel refreshed afterwards?

I also tell people that what they eat affects how their heart works. A balanced diet helps the blood vessels leading from the heart stay open and clean. Blood vessels take the pumped blood to the body and bring it oxygen. A poor diet can lead to fatty deposits in the blood vessels. The deposits clog them up. Vessels full of clogged-up deposits make it hard for the heart to pump blood through. Clogged vessels also limit the amount of blood and oxygen reaching the body.

Exercise and a well-balanced diet are important parts of keeping your heart and blood vessels healthy. A healthy heart and blood vessel system make us all feel more energetic. They allow us to do all of our daily activities more efficiently.

Now answer Numbers 13 through 18. Base your answers on the articles "Good Health" and "Advice for a Healthy Heart."

13 Read this sentence from the article "Good Health."

> **The blood contains oxygen, which reaches every part of the body by coursing through blood vessels.**

Why does the author use the word *coursing* instead of the word *going* in the sentence above?

- Ⓐ to show that the blood flows rapidly
- Ⓑ to show that the blood is full of oxygen
- Ⓒ to show the path in which the blood flows
- Ⓓ to show how the blood trickles through the blood vessels

14 Which BEST describes how the author organizes ideas in the article "Good Health"?

- Ⓕ description
- Ⓖ cause and effect
- Ⓗ chronological order
- Ⓘ comparison/contrast

15 How does the author organize ideas in paragraph 2 of the article "Advice for a Healthy Heart"?

- Ⓐ The author describes the size, color, shape, and structure of the heart.
- Ⓑ The author compares the heart to other types of muscles in the human body.
- Ⓒ The author describes the sequence of events that happen in the body as the heart beats.
- Ⓓ The author explains some of the problems that can develop as a result of too little exercise.

16 Read this sentence from the article "Advice for a Healthy Heart."

Did you feel refreshed afterwards?

What does the word *refreshed* mean in the sentence above?

- Ⓕ done with great skill
- Ⓖ having recently arrived
- Ⓗ appreciative or thankful for
- Ⓘ given new strength or energy

17 Which of the following BEST explains why the article "Advice for a Healthy Heart" tells more about heart health than the article "Good Health"?

- Ⓐ It is written by an expert on the human heart and heart health.
- Ⓑ It is written by a patient seeking information on how the heart works.
- Ⓒ It is written to help doctors learn a new way of treating patients' hearts.
- Ⓓ It is written like a story, describing how the heart works from the heart's point of view.

18 Given the information in BOTH articles, why is exercise important to good health?

- Ⓕ Exercise helps your brain function better when solving difficult problems.
- Ⓖ Exercise is a fun activity that can be shared among friends and family members.
- Ⓗ Exercise makes the heart stronger and more efficient and gives you more energy.
- Ⓘ Exercise prevents fatty deposits from forming in and clogging your blood vessels.

Read the passage "A Tree Needs a Special Place" before answering Numbers 19 through 24.

A Tree Needs a Special Place

by Lyda Williamson
illustrated by Laura Jacobsen

Oscar leaped up onto the porch and bounded into the house. He unzipped his backpack, pulled out a plastic bag, and ran to find *Mamá*.

"Mamá, look!" shouted Oscar. He opened the bag to reveal a baby tree, roots and all. "We got them at school for Arbor Day."

"How exciting!" said Mamá.

Oscar looked at the tree. "But I don't know where to plant it."

Mamá smiled. "It needs a special place. When we moved here from Mexico, I was a little girl. I didn't have any friends. Our new house had a big backyard with an oak tree. My father hung a swing from it, and I'd swing for hours. One day, a little girl came over and asked if she could swing with me. It was Claudia."

Oscar nodded. Claudia was Mamá's best friend. "Maybe someday this tree will grow big enough for a swing," he said. "I'll go show *Abuelito* and *Abuelita*!"

Oscar sprinted downstairs to his grandparents' apartment.

Abuelito, Oscar's grandfather, opened the door. "¡*Hola*, Oscar!"

"Look, Abuelito! I got a tree at school for Arbor Day," Oscar said. "But I don't know where to plant it. We don't have a big backyard like Mamá did."

Abuelito smoothed back his graying hair. "No, but we'll find a place for it," he said. He squatted down to look at the tree. "Back in Mexico, the sun is so strong at midday that everyone must take a break. A huge paloverde tree grew at the edge of our cornfield. I loved to rest in its shade."

Abuelita laughed. "I can still picture you there!" She put her hand on Oscar's shoulder. "Let me tell you about my favorite trees," she said. "My mamá loved to make *agua de limón*. It's like lemonade, but it's made with limes. Lime trees grew everywhere in my town! Mamá would send me out to pick the limes, then she'd let me stir the water, juice, and sugar. We'd use colorful straws to sip our cool green drinks."

Name _____ Date _____

"Mmmm, sounds good," said Oscar.

"I'll make it for you sometime," said Abuelita. "Now go find a spot to plant *your* tree."

"I will!" said Oscar. He raced up the steps and out the front door. Just as he stepped onto the porch, *Papá* pulled up in his car.

"What do you have there?" asked Papá.

Oscar showed him the tree.

Papá smiled. "When I was a boy in Michigan, my father would always make guacamole with avocados from the store.

Oscar nodded. He liked the tasty green dip.

"He'd mix it up and talk about Mexico. One time he saved the avocado seed. We put it in water. Every day, I watched it. Soon a tiny green sprout appeared. It became a baby tree. We nursed it along, then planted it in the ground."

"Did avocados grow on it, Papá?" asked Oscar.

"No, it couldn't survive the cold winter," Papa said. "But I'll always remember that special time with my father."

Oscar's sister walked up the sidewalk toward them.

"Magdalena, look!" Oscar held up the tree. "But I need a place to plant it."

"Let's see," said Magdalena. "At our old house, when you were a baby, a huge poplar tree grew near our sidewalk. It was taller than every other tree around. Wherever I was in town, I could always see our tree high above everything else."

Oscar glanced at the wide strip of grass between their sidewalk and the street. It was the perfect place! "Thanks, Magdalena—I'm going to plant my tree right here."

The sun was beginning to set. By now, the rest of Oscar's family had come outside to see where Oscar would plant his tree.

Oscar read the planting directions. "'Every fall this sugar maple will turn a brilliant red-orange. To plant it, dig a hole twice the size of the roots. Place the roots in the hole, and fill it with dirt. Water the tree often for the first year.'"

Abuelito got the shovel. Mamá got the watering can.

Name _____ Date _____

"Ready, Oscar?" asked Papá.

"I'm ready!" Oscar looked around at his family and grinned. "We'll have a beautiful tree right in front of our house for all of us to enjoy.

Papá dug a hole. Oscar held the tree in place as Magdalena, Abuelita, and Abuelito gently pushed dirt around it. When they were finished, Mamá sprinkled water on top.

Everyone stood back to admire the new tree. Oscar couldn't wait to watch it grow.

Name _____ Date _____

**Now answer Numbers 19 through 24. Base your answers on the passage
"A Tree Needs a Special Place."**

19 Read this sentence from the passage.

> **Oscar leaped up onto the porch and bounded into the house.**

Which word means almost the SAME as the word *bounded* in the
sentence above?

Ⓐ bounced

Ⓑ hid

Ⓒ strolled

Ⓓ trembled

20 Read these sentences from the passage.

> **"Mamá, look!" shouted Oscar. He opened the bag to reveal a
> baby tree, roots and all.**

What does the author's choice of words reveal about Oscar in the
sentences above?

Ⓕ He is upset.

Ⓖ He is excited.

Ⓗ He is relaxed.

Ⓘ He is frightened.

21 What is Oscar's problem with his tree?

Ⓐ He thinks it is too small to survive.

Ⓑ He fears his family will not want it.

Ⓒ He is unsure about where to plant it.

Ⓓ He cannot read the directions for planting.

Name _____ Date _____

22 What happens BEFORE Oscar hears his family's stories about their special trees?

- Ⓕ He gets his own tree from school.

- Ⓖ He plants his tree with his family.

- Ⓗ He decides where to plant the tree.

- Ⓘ He reads the directions for planting.

23 What can the reader conclude about Oscar's family members based on what happens in the passage?

- Ⓐ None of them have ever planted a tree before.

- Ⓑ They each have a fond memory of a particular tree.

- Ⓒ They are all too busy with their own activities to help Oscar.

- Ⓓ They have different ideas about where Oscar should plant his tree.

24 Where does Oscar plant his tree?

- Ⓕ in their backyard

- Ⓖ next to the sidewalk

- Ⓗ on the other side of town

- Ⓘ at the edge of a cornfield

Read the passage "Ben Liang's Story" before answering Numbers 25 through 30.

Ben Liang's Story

Ben Liang slumped over at his desk in school. He stared down at a blank piece of paper in front of him, worrying about his latest homework assignment. His teacher, Ms. Valdez, had just said to the class, "For the past couple of weeks, we have been reading stories about family, adventures, and pets. Today I want each of you to write a story about your family, an adventure, or a pet." Ben's spirits fell. He had no idea what to write about! He contemplated his story's topic as he gazed at the sheet of white paper.

Ben and his family had moved to America from China when he was still a toddler. His father and mother purchased a small Chinese restaurant. The apartment upstairs became home to Ben, his father and mother, his grandmother, and his younger sister, Emily. Before he began attending his new school, Ben enjoyed helping his mother and grandmother fold dumplings for their customers. While they prepared the food, they would practice speaking English together. Ben thought that this cherished time with his family might make a good story.

Or Ben could write about feasting on dim sum every week with his family and friends. Dim sum was his favorite Chinese meal. Dim sum included Chinese dumplings, delicious meat dishes, and lots of fresh, hot vegetables. In Chinese, *dim sum* means "a little bit of the heart." Ben thought that was an excellent name because the foods on the dim sum table are made from the heart.

On dim sum days, Ben and his cousins played among the empty tables in his parents' restaurant before the customers arrived. One morning, the children quietly opened the kitchen door to watch the cooks making dim sum. Suddenly one cook collided with a cart full of food. Everything went crashing to the floor. Everyone went running to the kitchen to help. Ben and his relatives worked hard all that day to make more food. Ben smiled as he recalled the dim sum incident. He thought that perhaps Ms. Valdez would enjoy reading that story.

Then Ben remembered one special Sunday when his father took him along with his mother, sister, and grandmother to a nearby park for a day of relaxation. In the center of the park was a big lake surrounded by tall, green pine trees. Ben's father rented a rowboat and took Ben and Emily out on the lake.

Ben heard his mother shout, "Look, turtles!" She pointed. Ben's father started rowing in that direction. There, near the bank of the lake, dozens of turtles were visible.

Name _____ Date _____

"Let's catch one," Ben's father suggested. Ben and Emily nodded eagerly. As Ben's father rowed nearer to the swimming creatures, Ben reached over the side of the boat to seize one of the biggest turtles.

"I got it!" he yelled, scooping the turtle into the boat.

"He's huge," giggled Emily. She turned to her father and asked, "Can we keep him?"

Ben's father laughed. "Sure we can," he said. "We can put him in the wading pool I bought for you and Ben a couple of years ago. You will have to be responsible. You will need to take very good care of him and think of a name for him."

What an adventure that had been! Ben smiled to himself. He was thinking that he still had that turtle, and it was the greatest pet he'd ever owned. He had named his turtle Dim Sum because he thought his pet was a "bit of the heart," just like his favorite family meal.

Ben eventually began to relax as he started writing his assignment for Ms. Valdez. The title of his story would be "Dim Sum: My Pet Turtle."

_____

Now answer Numbers 25 through 30. Base your answers on the passage "Ben Liang's Story."

25 Why is Ben unhappy at the beginning of the passage?

   Ⓐ   His teacher is boring him.

   Ⓑ   He does not like sitting at his desk.

   Ⓒ   He does not know what to write about.

   Ⓓ   His father has purchased a Chinese restaurant.

Name _____ Date _____

26 Which of the following topics does Ben FIRST consider writing about?

Ⓕ catching a turtle at the lake

Ⓖ making dim sum at the restaurant

Ⓗ practicing English with his family

Ⓘ playing with his cousins in the restaurant

27 Read this sentence from the passage.

There, near the bank of the lake, dozens of turtles were visible.

What does the Latin root *vis* mean in the word *visible* in the sentence above?

Ⓐ light

Ⓑ pull

Ⓒ see

Ⓓ turn

28 Read this sentence from the passage.

You will have to be responsible.

What does the word *responsible* mean in the sentence above?

Ⓕ loving

Ⓖ trustworthy

Ⓗ able to be done

Ⓘ can be reasoned with

29 Why is the lake important to the passage?

Ⓐ The lake is full of turtles.

Ⓑ The family eats dim sum at the lake.

Ⓒ It is a special Sunday for Ben's family.

Ⓓ Ben gets his idea for the story because of the lake.

30 Which detail from the passage BEST explains what Ben will write about?

Ⓕ "What an adventure that had been!"

Ⓖ "He was thinking that he still had that turtle…"

Ⓗ "The title of his story would be 'Dim Sum: My Pet Turtle.'"

Ⓘ "He had named his turtle Dim Sum because he thought his pet was a 'bit of the heart'…"

Read the article "All About Robots" before answering Numbers 31 through 35.

All About Robots

Did you know that you have robots in your home? Every time an alarm clock blares you are hearing a robot. When your mother puts food in the microwave, she is using a robot. When you put a movie in to watch, you are using a robot. Robots have many uses.

What is a robot? A robot is a machine that can do work that is normally done by people. The robot is run by a computer, which acts as its "brain." The brain tells the robot what to do.

Robots do many jobs that people do not want to do. They build cars, make parts for machines, and even make candy bars. Many companies use robots because they never get sick, they do not need to eat, and they never have to rest.

Some robots do jobs that are not safe for people to do. For example, because the planet Mars would be a dangerous place to visit, scientists sent robots, instead of people, to check out Mars. The robots gathered important information about Mars and then relayed that information back to Earth. This helps everyone to know more about the red planet.

Robots can go other places that would not be safe for people. They can go into burning buildings and help extinguish fires. Scientists use robots to go inside volcanoes and study what is happening. Robots can also be used to learn about the ocean because they can dive far deeper than people. They gather information about fish and plants that people have never seen before.

Soon robots may be used for even more important jobs. They could help police, doctors, farmers, and families. Yes, there may be even more robots in your home. Robots to help you clean the house and even make you lemonade!

Look at the chart to learn about some of the early advances in robot history.

Early Advances in Robotics

Year	Inventor	Nationality	Invention(s)
350 B.C.	Archytas	Greek	Mechanical bird
About 200 B.C.	Ctesibus	Greek	Water clocks
1495	Leonardo DaVinci	Italian	Knight in armor
1738	Jacques de Vaucanson	French	Two musical players and a duck
1770	Pierre and Henri-Louis Jaquet-Droz	Swiss	Three dolls

Now answer Numbers 31 through 35. Base your answers on the article "All About Robots."

31 What does the author use to introduce the definition of the word *robot*?

Ⓥ italics

ⓑ a question

ⓔ underlining

ⓖ an exclamation

Name _____ Date _____

32 Read this sentence from the article.

The brain tells the robot what to do.

What does the word *brain* mean in the sentence above?

Ⓕ the front part of the head

Ⓖ the device to control functions

Ⓗ a person who is a good planner

Ⓘ a person who is very intelligent

33 Which of the following does the author use to support the point that some robots do jobs that are unsafe for people to do?

Ⓐ A microwave is one type of robot.

Ⓑ Some robots are used to build cars.

Ⓒ Some robots can make machine parts.

Ⓓ Some robots are sent inside volcanoes.

34 Which column of the chart could the reader use to find out which inventor was Italian?

Ⓕ Year

Ⓖ Inventor

Ⓗ Nationality

Ⓘ Invention(s)

35 According to the chart, how are Archytas and Ctesibus ALIKE?

Ⓐ Both have the same last name.

Ⓑ Both shared the same nationality.

Ⓒ Both invented something musical.

Ⓓ Both made inventions in the same year.

Revising and Editing

Read the introduction and the passage "A Day on the Farm" before answering Numbers 1 through 7.

Elise wrote this passage about life on a farm. Read her passage and think about the changes she should make.

A Day on the Farm

(1) On a typical morning, you probably wake up, get dressed, and go to school. (2) I do all these things too, and more. (3) During the week my sister and I wake up before the sun rises and start working immediately. (4) That's because my family lives on a farm. (5) It has been in our family since the civil war.

(6) First, we feed our pets, Max the dog and Henry the cat. (7) Then we put on boots and walk to the barn. (8) Most mornings we must used a flashlight to find our way. (9) We feed both the chickens and the dairy cows. (10) It is important to make sure all of the animals have plenty of water and clean stalls. (11) Our last chore is to gather the eggs from the chicken coop for breakfast. (12) Yesterday we taked 12 fresh eggs back to the house.

(13) After we've finished our morning chores, we eat breakfast with Mom and Dad. (14) Then we put on our backpacks and walk to the bus stop.

(15) While we are at school, Mom and Dad completes the remainder of the chores. (16) They take care of the fields where we grow corn and beans.

(17) When my sister and I arrive home from school, we do our homework and eat a healthful snack. (18) Then we have time to play. (19) Afterward, we eat

dinner together. (20) We always go to bed early. (21) Our life on the farm

may be busier than most people's, but we keep usselves entertained!

_____

Now answer Numbers 1 through 7. Base your answers on the changes Elise should make.

1 What change should be made in sentence 5?

Ⓐ change *has been* to **have being**

Ⓑ change *our* to **their**

Ⓒ insert a comma after *family*

Ⓓ change *civil war* to **Civil War**

2 What change should be made in sentence 8?

Ⓕ change *morning* to **mornings**

Ⓖ change *must used* to **must use**

Ⓗ insert a comma after *flashlight*

Ⓘ change *a* to **an**

3 What change should be made in sentence 12?

Ⓐ insert *have* after **we**

Ⓑ change *taked* to **took**

Ⓒ change *fresh* to **freshest**

Ⓓ insert a comma after *eggs*

Name _____   Date _____

4 Which sentence could BEST follow and support sentence 14?

(F) I got a new backpack last week because my old one wore out.

(G) One of our cows has a new calf, and it needs a lot of attention.

(H) My mother and father went to my school when they were children.

(I) The school bus picks us up, and we arrive at school just before the bell rings.

5 What change should be made in sentence 15?

(A) change *we* to **they**

(B) delete the comma after *school*

(C) change *completes* to **complete**

(D) change *chores* to **chore**

6 Which revision should be made in sentences 19 and 20?

(F) Afterward, we eat dinner together, we always go to bed early

(G) Afterward, we eat dinner together, or we always go to bed early.

(H) Afterward, we eat dinner together, and we always go to bed early.

(I) Afterward, we eat dinner together then we always go to bed early.

7 What change should be made in sentence 21?

(A) insert a comma after *farm*

(B) change *busier* to **busyer**

(C) delete the comma after **people's**

(D) change *usselves* to **ourselves**

Name _____ Date _____

Read the introduction and the article "Bats" before answering Numbers 8 through 14.

Sam wrote this article about bats. Read his article and think about the changes he should make.

Bats

(1) Some people thought that bats are scary, but they are actually interesting, helpful animals. (2) Bats are mammals. (3) In fact, they are the only mammals that can truly fly. (4) This is just one interesting fact about bats. (5) The more you know about bats, the more you realize how fascinating they is.

(6) Insects are the ones who should be afraid of bats. (7) Some bats can eat their own wait in insects in one night. (8) That's a skill you might be thankful for if you've ever had an itchy mosquito bite. (9) Poison ivy can also make you itch.

(10) Some bats fertilize plants as they fly from one plant to another, feeding on the nectar and pollen of flowers. (11) Bats scatter plant seeds as they fly, too. (12) Both of these actions. (13) Help new plants to grow.

(14) When it comes to finding they're way around, bats have an unusual set of skills. (15) Many types of bats do not see well, so they use their

hearing in a very special way to help them "see" things. (16) Bats make high-pitched sounds and listen to the echoes as the sounds bounce off of objects. (17) Bats use this unusual method of seeing as they go very, very fast through the air and hunt at night. (18) Next time you is walking around outside at dusk, look up and see if you can spot your fellow mammal, the bat!

Now answer Numbers 8 through 14. Base your answers on the changes Sam should make.

8 What change should be made in sentence 1?

   Ⓕ   change *people* to **peoples**

   Ⓖ   change *thought* to **think**

   Ⓗ   change *but* to **and**

   Ⓘ   change *interesting* to **interest**

9 What change should be made in sentence 5?

   Ⓐ   change *know* to **knew**

   Ⓑ   insert a period after *bats*

   Ⓒ   change *fascinating* to *fascinated*

   Ⓓ   change *is* to **are**

10 What change should be made in sentence 7?

   Ⓕ   change *eat* to **eating**

   Ⓖ   change *their* to **they're**

   Ⓗ   change *wait* to **weight**

   Ⓘ   change *insects* to **insectes**

11 What change should be made in sentence 14?

Ⓐ change *to* to **too**

Ⓑ change *they're* to **their**

Ⓒ insert a comma after *bats*

Ⓓ change *have* to **has**

12 Which sentence does NOT belong in the article?

Ⓕ sentence 3

Ⓖ sentence 9

Ⓗ sentence 11

Ⓘ sentence 16

13 What change is needed in sentence 17?

Ⓐ change *use* to **used**

Ⓑ change *unusual* to **unusually**

Ⓒ insert a period after *seeing*

Ⓓ change *go very, very fast* to **speed**

14 What change should be made in sentence 18?

Ⓕ change *is* to **are**

Ⓖ delete the comma after *dusk*

Ⓗ change *can* to **could**

Ⓘ change *your* to **you're**

Read the introduction and the passage "My Family" before answering Numbers 15 through 20.

Darcy wrote this passage about her grandparents. Read her passage and think about the changes she should make.

My Family

(1) If you could go anywhere in the world, where will you go?

(2) I would go either to Italy and Japan. (3) That is because my grandmother is from Japan and my grandfather is from Italy. (4) They meeted in the United States more than 50 years ago.

(5) I love visiting my grandparents. (6) Seeing them always reminds me of our unique heritage. (7) My grandmother like to make many of the dishes she ate as a child in Japan. (8) My favorite food she makes is called katsudon, a dish that has rice, egg, and meat.

(9) I always see my grandmother on May 5. (10) On that day, we celebrate a japanese holiday called Children's Day, to recognize the happiness of children. (11) My grandmother hangs a brightly colored kite in the shape of a fish outside my door.

(12) My grandfather enjoy sharing his heritage with me, too. (13) Every time we see him. (14) He kisses each family member twice, once on each cheek. (15) Like my grandmother, he enjoys cooking foods from his childhood. (16) He has taught me how to make pasta.

Now answer Numbers 15 through 20. Base your answers on the changes Darcy should make.

15 What change should be made in sentence 1?

  Ⓐ change *world* to **worlds**

  Ⓑ insert a comma after *where*

  Ⓒ change *will* to **would**

  Ⓓ change the question mark to a period

16 What change should be made in sentence 4?

  Ⓕ change *meeted* to **met**

  Ⓖ change *United States* to **united states**

  Ⓗ change *than* to **then**

  Ⓘ change *years* to **year**

17 What change should be made in sentence 7?

  Ⓐ change *like* to **likes**

  Ⓑ change *make* to **makes**

  Ⓒ change *ate* to **eat**

  Ⓓ insert a comma after *child*

18 What change should be made in sentence 10?

  Ⓕ delete the comma after *day*

  Ⓖ change *japanese* to **Japanese**

  Ⓗ change *Children's* to *children's*

  Ⓘ change *happiness* to **happyness**

Name _____ Date _____

19 Which sentence could BEST follow and support sentence 11?

Ⓐ Once I entered a kite-flying contest.

Ⓑ My favorite holiday is Thanksgiving.

Ⓒ My grandmother is a really good cook.

Ⓓ The fish represents courage and strength.

20 What revision is needed in sentences 13 and 14?

Ⓕ Every time we see him, kisses each family member twice, once on each cheek.

Ⓖ Every time we see him, he kisses each family member twice, once on each cheek.

Ⓗ Every time we see him, he kisses each family member twice. Once on each cheek.

Ⓘ Every time we see him, and he kisses each family member twice, once on each cheek.

Name _____ Date _____

Writing Opinions

Read the prompt and plan your response.

> Your town is trying to promote itself as a great place to live.
>
> Think about some of the things that make your town a great place to live.
>
> Now write to persuade someone that your town is a great place to live.

Use this space to make your notes before you begin writing. The writing on this page will NOT be scored.

_____

_____

_____

_____

_____

_____

_____

_____

Name _____ Date _____

Begin writing your response here. The writing on this page and the next page WILL be scored.

_____

_____

_____

_____

_____

_____

_____

_____

_____

_____

_____

_____

_____

_____

_____

Name _____ Date _____

_____

_____

_____

_____

_____

_____

_____

_____

_____

_____

_____

_____

_____

_____

_____

Reading Complex Text

Read the brochure "The La Brea Tar Pits" and the journal entry "Lessons from La Brea." As you read, stop and answer each question. Use evidence from the brochure and the journal entry to support your answers.

The La Brea Tar Pits

Looking for an interesting trip for your next vacation? Look no further than the La Brea Tar Pits. Located in California, the La Brea Tar Pits are famous for their astonishing variety of plant and animal fossils. Fossils in the La Brea Tar Pits can be up to 40,000 years old. Over the last hundred years, scientists have uncovered over three million fossils at the La Brea Tar Pits. Many of these fossils are on display there. You can see the remains of a 10,000-pound Columbian mammoth, an 11-foot tall short-faced bear, and a saber-toothed cat, the official state fossil of California.

---

❶ How do the details in the above paragraph support the author's point that the La Brea Tar Pits would be an interesting place to visit?

_____

_____

_____

Why are the La Brea Tar Pits home to so many fossils? Quite simply, all of the organisms found there have at one point gotten stuck there. The pits are full of a thick, oozing substance. Often called tar, this substance is actually natural asphalt. It comes from an underground reservoir, or pool, made of crude oil. The crude oil mixes with sand, stone, dirt, leaves, and other organic material to form something like quicksand.

The pits often appear as solid ground. However, particularly during warm days, the ground can turn soft and sticky. An animal wandering over one of the pits could get stuck. The trapped animal would often

Name _____ Date _____

attract predators, usually large animals that eat other animals. These predators could also become trapped. In addition, passing scavengers would frequent the tar pits. If they were unlucky, they could become trapped, too! All of the animals would then sink deeper into the pits. There, the pits would preserve and protect them from the normal processes of erosion.

Once the animals died, the softer parts of their bodies, such as skin, muscle, and fur, would decay. The bones and teeth, however, remained intact. These parts would absorb asphalt from the tar pits, which would strengthen them and keep them from decaying. Sediment washed into the pits by rain would help keep the fossils buried.

2 Why are so many large animal fossils found at La Brea? Provide one example from the section above to support your answer.

_____

_____

_____

Fortunately for you, you don't have to unearth these fossils yourself. The Page Museum at the La Brea Tar Pits contains thousands of fossils. Come visit the La Brea Tar Pits! It's a great way to travel thousands of years into the past *without* a time machine.

Name _____ Date _____

Lessons from La Brea

Dear Journal,

Yesterday, our class went on a field trip to the Rancho La Brea Tar Pits in Los Angeles. I have lived near Los Angeles my whole life. But I never knew that the La Brea Tar Pits existed until last week! It's strange to imagine mammoths and saber-toothed cats roaming where there are now highways and shopping centers. Visiting La Brea felt like stepping out of present-day life and into the Ice Age.

Before the field trip, we spent several days learning about the La Brea Tar Pits. It's amazing how many fossils have been found there! Our teacher explained that the tar is not actually the substance used to pave roads. It is really natural asphalt. We learned about how the tar pits formed. We also learned about how animals got stuck in the tar pits in the first place.

Our first stop on the field trip was the Page Museum. A tour guide led us around different displays of fossils recovered from the tar pits. The first thing I noticed about the fossils is that they were brown! I had thought that fossilized bones would be white. After all, the dinosaur bones I saw at the natural history museum were white. I learned, though, that there was a very good explanation for why the fossils from the La Brea Tar Pits were brown.

Our guide explained what had happened to the animals that had been trapped in the tar pits. After they died, their bodies would eventually break down. Only their bones and teeth would be left. According to our guide, if the bones had been left out in the hot Los Angeles sun, they would have broken down over time. They would have turned to dust. Instead, the natural asphalt in the tar pits helped preserve the bones, or keep them unchanged. How? Well, just like our skin, bones have tiny holes in them. These holes are called pores. Over thousands of years, the dark, sticky asphalt would seep into the pores in the animals' bones. This helped the bones become stronger. It made them more resistant to decay. It also explains why the bones turned brown!

3 Based on the information in "The La Brea Tar Pits" and "Lessons from La Brea," explain how fossils in the tar pits were preserved.

_____

_____

_____

There wasn't enough time in the day to explore everything I wanted to at the La Brea Tar Pits. I definitely want to go back during the summer. Then, I can watch the scientists digging for fossils in one of the pits. Maybe, just maybe, they'll need a volunteer assistant.

Until next time, Journal!

Chris

---

4 How are the brochure and the journal entry similar in the information they provide? How are they different in the way the two authors present the information?

_____

_____

_____

_____

_____

Reading and Analyzing Text

Read the passages "Help for Dogs" and "The Hike" before answering Numbers 1 through 18.

Help for Dogs

Joseph worked to raise money for an animal shelter. He wrote about his experience in a journal. Here is part of Joseph's journal.

March 14—Today a piece of mail caught my eye. My mom opened the envelope, glanced at the paper, and tossed it into the recycling bin. I saw pictures of dogs, so I pulled it out of the bin and read it. The paper was from a local animal shelter, and it showed dogs that had been rescued and were in need of a good home. The letter that accompanied the pictures explained that the shelter was in need of money to pay for dog food, medicine, and other bills. I want to help the dogs at the shelter.

March 15—I showed the letter from the animal shelter to my friend Carlos. He said that he wanted to help, too. It gave me the idea of asking everyone in the neighborhood to help raise money for the shelter. My mother said I should come up with a plan and present it to Mrs. Young, the head of the local community center. I scheduled an appointment to talk to Mrs. Young tomorrow after school.

March 16—I proposed my idea to Mrs. Young, and she loved it! We're going to have a family game night at the center. People will bring games to play with other families, and we will charge five dollars per family to attend. We will sell snacks, too. Of course, people can donate more money if they would like. I have a lot of planning and organizing to do in order to launch this event in just over two weeks!

April 2—Family game night is tomorrow! Today after school I set up everything in the community center's cafeteria. I hope that many families will attend. I asked a newspaper reporter to come, too, to take pictures of the event. I hope that the publicity will inspire other people in the community to give a donation to the shelter.

April 4—I am proud to announce that game night was extremely successful! Thirty-seven families came to play games, and we were able to raise almost $300 for the animal shelter. I'm very excited to give them the money.

Name _____ Date _____

The Hike

*Tamara faced a challenge she did not think she could overcome. She
wrote about her feelings in her journal. Here is part of Tamara's journal.*

February 4—Everyone is excited about our field trip tomorrow—everyone
except for me, that is. We're going to a park where there is a climbing rock with
trails that lead you from the ground to the almost 500-feet high summit[1].

The climbing rock may as well be the gigantic Mount Everest! There is no
way I'll reach the top of it. Though I'd like to be an athlete, I just don't seem
to have the skills for most sports. My legs refuse to carry me very fast when I
run. My absolute least favorite time of day is gym. When Coach Case begins to
describe a game, I slowly try to make myself invisible so I don't have to play.
Maybe I'll wake up sick and have to stay home tomorrow.

February 5—You will not believe what happened today! I actually made
it to the summit all by myself! I believe it may have been the most rewarding
experience of my life so far. Let me tell you all about it.

First, I woke up and tried to tell Mom I was too sick to go to school. She eyed
me suspiciously as she took my temperature. Of course, it was normal, so she
would not let me stay home. As soon as I arrived at school, the teacher checked
to be sure we all had our hats, water bottles, and sunscreen. I got on the school
bus with a heavy heart and took a seat next to my friend Anita. Soon we were at
the park and getting off of the bus.

With water bottles in hand, we gathered at the bottom of the rock to start the
hike. The guides made sure we were all wearing our safety helmets correctly.
I decided to be like the tortoise instead of the hare and take a slow and steady
pace. As I started the hike, I saw interesting rock formations and unusual
reptiles. When I saw other kids stopping to catch their breath, I realized that I felt
fine; in fact, I felt fantastic! I continued my slow, steady climb until I reached the
top. I felt like I was on top of the world! I never wanted to come down.

After about 30 minutes, it was time to start our descent. I caught myself
skipping down the trail. My heart swelled with pride as I thought about what I'd
accomplished. Watch out, Mount Everest, here I come!

[1] **summit:** the highest point

Name _____ Date _____

Now answer Numbers 1 through 18. Base your answers on the passages "Help for Dogs" and "The Hike."

1 Read this sentence from the passage "Help for Dogs."

The letter that accompanied the pictures explained that the shelter was in need of money to pay for dog food, medicine, and other bills.

What word has the SAME sound for *c* as the word *medicine*?

Ⓐ advice

Ⓑ fabric

Ⓒ jacket

Ⓓ peaches

2 What inspires Joseph to want to help the dogs at the animal shelter in the passage "Help for Dogs"?

Ⓕ He attends an event at the animal shelter with his family.

Ⓖ He reads an article about the shelter in the local newspaper.

Ⓗ His friend Carlos tells him about a fundraiser he is organizing.

Ⓘ He reads a letter about dogs at the animal shelter that are in need.

3 Read the dictionary entry below.

---
head /hed/ *noun* **1.** the part of the body containing the brain, eyes, ears, nose, and mouth. **2.** mental ability. **3.** the main side of a coin. **4.** the person who leads or is in charge of something.

Read this sentence from the passage "Help for Dogs."

> **My mother said I should come up with a plan and present it to Mrs. Young, the head of the local community center.**

Which meaning BEST fits the way the word *head* is used in the sentence above?

Ⓐ meaning 1

Ⓑ meaning 2

Ⓒ meaning 3

Ⓓ meaning 4

4 Read this sentence from the passage "Help for Dogs."

> **I scheduled an appointment to talk to Mrs. Young tomorrow after school.**

What does the word *appointment* mean in the sentence above?

Ⓕ game

Ⓖ job

Ⓗ meeting

Ⓘ practice

5 Read this sentence from the passage "Help for Dogs."

> **I proposed my idea to Mrs. Young, and she loved it!**

What does the word *proposed* mean in the sentence above?

Ⓐ asked for help

Ⓑ solved a problem

Ⓒ suggested a course of action

Ⓓ organized a community event

6 Read this sentence from the passage "Help for Dogs."

> **Of course, people can donate more money if they would like.**

What word has the SAME sound for *t* as the word *donate*?

- (F) capture
- (G) latch
- (H) motion
- (I) waited

7 Read this sentence from the passage "Help for Dogs."

> **I hope that the publicity will inspire other people in the community to give a donation to the shelter.**

What does the word *publicity* mean in the sentence above?

- (A) an event designed to raise money for a cause
- (B) something meant to get the public's attention
- (C) something done in public to benefit neighbors
- (D) a desire to appear in a newspaper for others to see

8 Read the SAME sentence from the passage again.

> **I hope that the publicity will inspire other people in the community to give a donation to the shelter.**

What does the word *donation* mean in the sentence above?

- (F) time spent helping others
- (G) news printed in an article
- (H) money given to help others
- (I) pictures printed in the newspaper

Name _____ Date _____

9   What is the theme of the passage "Help for Dogs"?

Ⓐ   Any problem can be solved with money.

Ⓑ   It is exciting to both give and receive gifts.

Ⓒ   Pets can bring lots of joy into people's lives.

Ⓓ   People working together can make a big difference.

10   Read this sentence from the passage "The Hike."

My legs refuse to carry me very fast when I run.

Why does Tamara describe her legs as not willing to run fast?

Ⓕ   to suggest that she is trying to improve her running ability

Ⓖ   to show that a past injury causes her legs to hurt when she runs

Ⓗ   to suggest that no matter how hard she tries, she cannot run fast

Ⓘ   to show that she does not enjoy running, even though she is good at it

11   Read this sentence from the passage "The Hike."

**I got on the school bus with a heavy heart and took a seat next to
my friend Anita.**

Why does Tamara use the phrase *with a heavy heart* in the sentence above?

Ⓐ   to express her feelings of dread

Ⓑ   to show that she had a high fever

Ⓒ   to show how she was trying to gather her courage

Ⓓ   to imply that she was feeling excited about the hike

12 Read this sentence from the passage "The Hike."

> **I decided to be like the tortoise instead of the hare and take a slow and steady pace.**

How does this reference to the tortoise and the hare help the reader understand how Tamara is going to approach the hike?

- Ⓕ A slow, steady pace will give her plenty of time and space to face the hike.
- Ⓖ A slow, steady pace will guarantee that she beats her classmates to the summit.
- Ⓗ A slow, steady pace will ensure that she can hike alone and avoid her classmates.
- Ⓘ A slow, steady pace will allow her to waste time so she doesn't have to finish the hike.

13 Read this sentence from the passage "The Hike."

> **I caught myself skipping down the trail.**

Why does Tamara use the word *skipping* instead of the word *walking*?

- Ⓐ to show that she acts younger than her age
- Ⓑ to show that she feels happy about her success
- Ⓒ to show that she may have injured her leg on the hike
- Ⓓ to show how fast she goes down the trail compared to her pace going up

14 Read this sentence from the passage "The Hike."

> **My heart swelled with pride as I thought about what I'd accomplished.**

What does the word *swelled* mean in the sentence above?

- Ⓕ felt afraid
- Ⓖ became larger
- Ⓗ jumped in fear
- Ⓘ pounded heavily

Name _____ Date _____

15 Read this sentence from the passage "The Hike."

> **As I started the hike, I saw interesting rock formations and unusual reptiles.**

What does the word *unusual* mean in the sentence above?

- Ⓐ not common
- Ⓑ does not exist
- Ⓒ growing larger
- Ⓓ like something else

16 How are Tamara and Joseph ALIKE?

- Ⓕ They both defeat a fear.
- Ⓖ They both do something rewarding.
- Ⓗ They both do something to help others.
- Ⓘ They both think they will be unsuccessful.

17 What is one idea presented in BOTH passages?

- Ⓐ winning contests
- Ⓑ meeting new people
- Ⓒ overcoming challenges
- Ⓓ raising money for a cause

18 How are Joseph's feelings before the game night DIFFERENT from Tamara's feelings before the hike?

- Ⓕ Joseph feels nervous. Tamara feels calm.
- Ⓖ Joseph feels relaxed. Tamara feels bored.
- Ⓗ Joseph feels excited. Tamara feels unhappy.
- Ⓘ Joseph feels uncertain. Tamara feels confident.

Read the article "Solar Ovens Can Save the Day" before answering Numbers 19 through 35.

Solar Ovens Can Save the Day

Millions of people in developing countries do not have electricity. Many also lack readily available clean water. In order to produce safe food and water, people cut down trees or find other materials with which to make fire. If people treat polluted water or cook some foods over a fire, it can keep them from becoming ill. Unfortunately, making a fire from wood and other materials can lead to more problems. Cutting down trees ruins forests. Burning wood creates pollution. One way to overcome a number of these challenges is a solar oven. A solar oven offers a simple, convenient way to cook. Even better, it has little impact on the environment.

A solar oven is a box that performs like a regular oven. Instead of electricity, it is powered by a clean, natural source of energy: the sun. Solar ovens are designed to trap the sun's heat inside. This allows them to cook food or heat water inside. Temperatures inside solar ovens can climb to nearly 250 degrees Fahrenheit! If left in the sun long enough, a solar oven can cook all kinds of healthy foods. It can also boil water. This process can kill unsafe germs

in drinking water. Generally, solar ovens are made by using cardboard reflectors and a cooking box inside a layer of glass or plastic. The reflectors capture the sun's energy, directing it inside the oven. The plastic or glass layers trap the heat inside the box, just as in a regular oven. Since a solar oven doesn't burn fuel, it doesn't produce pollution.

Certainly, anyone can benefit from the use of a solar oven. By using only the sun's energy and creating no pollution, it has the word *green* written all over it! Initiatives in some of the world's developing regions have proven that solar ovens can benefit entire communities. People may spend hours finding, cutting, and carrying firewood. Then, they may spend even more time building and tending to a fire. A solar oven saves them lots of time and effort. They can simply prepare a meal and leave it in a solar oven. Their time can then be spent with family members or doing other activities. Furthermore, solar ovens are inexpensive (not to mention a piece of cake!) to build.

How to Build Your Own Solar Oven

You can find most of the supplies needed to build your solar oven around your house. You will need:

- A shoebox
- Aluminum foil
- Black construction paper
- Clear plastic wrap
- Scissors
- Tape

What to do:

1 First, cut a large rectangular flap out of the box lid. The flap should be almost as big as the top of the shoebox. Cut only three sides so that you can fold the flap back.

2 Tape foil to the inside of the flap. Then, cover and tape foil around the entire inside of the box as well. Make sure the shiny side of the foil is facing out. This will reflect the sun's rays.

3 Tape a piece of black construction paper to the inside bottom of the box, over the foil. The black color will absorb energy from the sun.

4 Tape several layers of plastic wrap over the opening you made in the shoebox lid in step one. This traps heat inside the box.

5 You have now built your solar oven. Now, place some food that you would like to heat up, such as soup, into the box.

6 Finally, open the flap and place your solar oven in direct sunlight. After a little while, you should hear the "hiss" of your dish cooking to completion. Enjoy!

Name _____ Date _____

Now answer Numbers 19 through 35. Base your answers on the article "Solar Ovens Can Save the Day."

19 Read this sentence from the article.

> **In order to produce safe food and water, people cut down trees or find other materials with which to make fire.**

What word has the same sound for *c* as the word *produce* in the sentence above?

Ⓐ advice

Ⓑ fabric

Ⓒ jacket

Ⓓ peaches

20 Read the dictionary entry below.

> **treat** /treet/ *verb* **1.** to deal with. **2.** to pay another's expenses. **3.** to present or discuss a subject. **4.** to apply a process to something, in order to improve it.

Read this sentence from the article.

> **If people treat polluted water or cook some foods over a fire, it can keep them from becoming ill.**

Which meaning BEST fits the way the word *treat* is used in the sentence above?

Ⓕ meaning 1

Ⓖ meaning 2

Ⓗ meaning 3

Ⓘ meaning 4

*Name _____ Date _____

21 Read this sentence from the article.

> **Unfortunately, making a fire from wood and other materials can lead to more problems.**

Which two guide words would MOST LIKELY be at the top of a dictionary page that has the word *unfortunately*?

- Ⓐ uneven • unfair
- Ⓑ unfit • unfriendly
- Ⓒ underneath • undo
- Ⓓ unhappy • unicorn

22 Read this sentence from the article.

> **One way to overcome a number of these challenges is a solar oven.**

What does the word *overcome* mean in the sentence above?

- Ⓕ affect
- Ⓖ conquer
- Ⓗ earn
- Ⓘ enter

23 Read this sentence from the article.

> **A solar oven is a box that performs like a regular oven.**

What does the word *performs* mean in the sentence above?

- Ⓐ does quickly
- Ⓑ carries out a task
- Ⓒ entertains with a show
- Ⓓ acts in an unusual way

Name _____ Date _____

24 Read this sentence from the article.

> **Temperatures inside solar ovens can climb to nearly 250 degrees Fahrenheit!**

Why does the author use the words *climb to* instead of the word *be* in the sentence above?

- Ⓕ to show the limits of a solar oven, in terms of what food it can cook

- Ⓖ to show how long it takes for a solar oven to heat food all the way through

- Ⓗ to show how effectively the sun's energy can raise the temperature of a solar oven

- Ⓘ to show how safe a solar oven is, since it cannot heat food beyond a certain temperature

25 Read this sentence from the article.

> **This process can kill unsafe germs in drinking water.**

What does the word *unsafe* mean in the sentence above?

- Ⓐ secure

- Ⓑ harmless

- Ⓒ dangerous

- Ⓓ not known

26 Which detail BEST supports the idea that solar ovens act like regular ovens?

- Ⓕ Burning wood can cause pollution.

- Ⓖ Many people do not have access to clean water.

- Ⓗ Solar ovens are designed to trap heat from the sun inside the oven.

- Ⓘ People in developing regions often spend lots of time gathering firewood.

27 Read this sentence from the article.

> **By using only the sun's energy and creating no pollution, it has the word *green* written all over it!**

What does the phrase *written all over* it imply in the sentence above?

- Ⓐ that solar ovens are especially green, or eco-friendly
- Ⓑ that solar ovens are currently very popular in the media
- Ⓒ that solar ovens are made of recyclable materials you can write on
- Ⓓ that solar ovens, while they seem eco-friendly, have drawbacks

28 Read this sentence from the article.

> **Initiatives in some of the world's developing regions have proven that solar ovens can benefit entire communities.**

What does the word *initiatives* mean in the sentence above?

- Ⓕ beginning projects
- Ⓖ adventurous journeys
- Ⓗ powers of government
- Ⓘ attitudes needed for success

29 Read this sentence from the article.

> **A solar oven saves them lots of time and effort.**

What is the CORRECT way to divide the word *effort* into syllables?

- Ⓐ e • ffort
- Ⓑ ef • fort
- Ⓒ eff • ort
- Ⓓ effo • rt

Name _____ Date _____

30 Read this sentence from article.

> **Furthermore, solar ovens are inexpensive (not to mention a piece of cake!) to build.**

What does the phrase *a piece of cake* mean in the sentence above?

- Ⓕ delicious

- Ⓖ very easy

- Ⓗ time-consuming

- Ⓘ involving many steps

31 Which detail BEST supports the idea that solar ovens are better for the environment?

- Ⓐ They don't create pollution.

- Ⓑ They can cook many types of food.

- Ⓒ They can benefit entire communities.

- Ⓓ They are made using cardboard reflectors.

32 Which BEST describes the overall structure of the article?

- Ⓕ description

- Ⓖ chronological order

- Ⓗ problem and solution

- Ⓘ comparison and contrast

33 Read this sentence from the section *How to Build Your Own Solar Oven*.

> **You can find most of the supplies needed to build your solar oven around your house.**

What does the word *supplies* mean in the sentence above?

(A) stored food

(B) necessary materials

(C) items available for purchase

(D) items that can be replaced by other items

34 Read this sentence from the section *How to Build Your Own Solar Oven*.

> **After a little while, you should hear the "hiss" of your dish cooking to completion.**

What effect does the author's use of the word *hiss* have on the reader?

(F) It suggests the sound the food makes as it cooks

(G) It gives the reader the sense that the solar oven is like a living thing.

(H) It gives the reader an idea of how long a solar oven takes to heat food.

(I) It implies that the food is not as good as it would be if made in a regular oven.

35 Which BEST describes how the author organizes ideas in the section *How to Build Your Own Solar Oven*?

(A) description

(B) comparison

(C) cause and effect

(D) chronological order

Revising and Editing

Read the introduction and the passage "Summer Vacation" before answering Numbers 1 through 7.

Myra wrote this passage about a vacation she took last summer. Read her passage and think about the changes she should make.

Summer Vacation

(1) Last summer, my dad decided that we should take an unusual vacation.

(2) I said I wanted to go to the beach, but Dad insisted on something else.

(3) He gave each of us an assignment. (4) My brothers and I had to find a

roadside attraction who we thought the family would enjoy. (5) It could not

be farther than 200 miles away from our home, and we could not share our

location with each other.

(6) About a week before our trip, each of us met secret with Dad.

(7) We gave him information around our chosen location. (8) Then he plotted

our route on a map.

(9) Finally, it was time. (10) We were all excited about the uncertainty

of the trip. (11) Where would we go? (12) What would we see?

(13) Our first stop was Austin's Cathedral of Junk. (14) My older

brother Erik Jr found this one. (15) Dad said he probably chose the

location because it reminded him of his intidy room. (16) Then we drove

south to Poteet where we saw the world's largest strawberry. (17) It was

made of metal, of course. (18) The next stop was a huge ice cream cone

in Port Isabel. (19) It was an ice cream shop in the shape of an ice cream

cone. (20) Dad surprised us with the last one. (21) It was a store on South

Padre Island. (22) The entrance was a huge shark with an open mouth.

(23) When we left the store, we went to the beach. (24) It was a vacation!

_____

**Now answer Numbers 1 through 7. Base your answers on the changes Myra
should make.**

❶ Which sentence could BEST be added after sentence 2?

    Ⓐ   Everyone in my family likes to eat ice cream.

    Ⓑ   We live in a small town outside Austin, Texas.

    Ⓒ   Some people enjoy going to the beach for vacation.

    Ⓓ   We would drive around Texas to see roadside attractions.

2 What change should be made in sentence 4?

Ⓕ change *had* to **have**

Ⓖ change *find* to **found**

Ⓗ change *who* to **that**

Ⓘ change *would* to **will**

3 What change should be made in sentence 6?

Ⓐ change *About* to **Into**

Ⓑ delete the comma after *trip*

Ⓒ change *secret* to **secretly**

Ⓓ change the period to a question mark

4 What change should be made in sentence 7?

Ⓕ change *We* to **They**

Ⓖ change *around* to **about**

Ⓗ change *our* to **are**

Ⓘ change *chosen* to **chose**

5 Which prepositional phrase could BEST be added to the end of sentence 9?

Ⓐ in our trip

Ⓑ for our trip

Ⓒ after our trip

Ⓓ about our trip

Name _____ Date _____

6 What change should be made in sentence 14?

   Ⓕ change *My* to **The**

   Ⓖ insert a comma after *older*

   Ⓗ insert a period after *Jr*

   Ⓘ change *this* to **that**

7 What change should be made in sentence 15?

   Ⓐ change *chose* to **choosed**

   Ⓑ change *because* to **until**

   Ⓒ change *him* to **he**

   Ⓓ change *intidy* to **untidy**

Read the introduction and the passage "The Winning Poem" before answering Numbers 8 through 14.

Manuel wrote this passage about something exciting that happened to him. Read his passage and think about the changes he should make.

The Winning Poem

(1) Have you ever entered a contest? (2) I've entered alot of them, but I never win. (3) At least I never won until now. (4) Recent, my friend, Julia, told me about a poetry-writing contest. (5) I love to write poetry, so I thought it would be a very, very nice contest for me.

(6) First, Mom and I used the Internet to read the rules on the contest's website. (7) Then I wrote the perfect poem. (8) I wrote a poem about writing poetry. (9) The poem is about how difficult it is to find just the right words and how wonderful it is to be able to express yourself through words in a poem. (10) I e-mailed the poem in the address on the Internet and tried to forget about the contest.

(11) After long six weeks, I received a reply. (12) I was so excited to read the letter, which began with the wonderful words, "Dear Mr Shaw, Congratulations!" (13) The envelope had a check for my winning poem, but the best part of all was seeing my poem in print in the magazine for everyone to read!

Now answer Numbers 8 through 14. Base your answers on the changes Manuel should make.

8   What change should be made in sentence 2?

    ⓕ   change *alot* to **a lot**

    ⓖ   delete the comma after *them*

    ⓗ   change *I* to **you**

    ⓘ   change *win* to **wins**

9   What change should be made to sentence 4?

    Ⓐ   change *Recent* to **Recently**

    Ⓑ   delete the comma after *Julia*

    Ⓒ   change *me* to **I**

    Ⓓ   change *about* to **around**

10   What change should be made in sentence 5?

    ⓕ   change *write* to **make**

    ⓖ   insert a comma after *thought*

    ⓗ   change *a very, very nice* to **the perfect**

    ⓘ   change *me* to **I**

11   Which sentence should be added after sentence 6?

    Ⓐ   Mom uses the computer for work sometimes.

    Ⓑ   This was the first writing contest I ever entered.

    Ⓒ   Julia was certain I had a good chance of winning.

    Ⓓ   When we were done, I wrote down ideas for a poem.

Name _____ Date _____

12 What change should be made in sentence 10?

- Ⓕ change *in* to **to**
- Ⓖ change *and* to **next**
- Ⓗ change *tried* to **try**
- Ⓘ change *forget* to **forgot**

13 What change should be made in sentence 11?

- Ⓐ After long six weeks, I received a reply.
- Ⓑ After long six weeks, I receive a reply.
- Ⓒ After, long six weeks I received a reply.
- Ⓓ After six long weeks, I received a reply.

14 What change should be made in sentence 12?

- Ⓕ change *excited* to **happy**
- Ⓖ change *which* to **and**
- Ⓗ insert a comma after *Dear*
- Ⓘ insert a period after *Mr*

Read the introduction and the passage "Rainbows" before answering Numbers 15 through 20.

Amelia wrote this passage about rainbows. Read her passage and think about the changes she should make.

Rainbows

(1) The light we usually see is called visible light. (2) Although this light may appear colorless or white, it is actually made up of different many colors, which are also called a spectrum. (3) In a spectrum, colors always appear in a specific order: red, orange, yellow, green, blue, indigo, and violet. (4) The easiest way to remember the colors of the visible spectrum is to remember the name Roy G Biv. (5) Each letter stands for a color—R is for red, O is for orange, Y is for yellow, G is for green, B is for blue, I is for indigo, and V is for violet. (6) These are the colors of a rainbow.

(7) Do you know what makes a rainbow? (8) Light passes through water, such as drops of rain, or a piece of glass. (9) The light bends or

Name _____ Date _____

splits, allowing you to see the different colors. (10) You normal see a

rainbow when it is raining and the sun is shining. (11) The sun will be

behind you and the rainbow in front to you. (12) Now when you see a

beautifull rainbow, you'll understand why it appears.

Now answer Numbers 15 through 20. Base your answers on the changes Amelia should make.

15 What change should be made in sentence 2?

Ⓐ change *Although* to **But**

Ⓑ change *made* to **make**

Ⓒ change *different many* to **many different**

Ⓓ change *called* to **calls**

16 What change should be made in sentence 4?

Ⓕ change *easiest* to **most easy**

Ⓖ change *colors* to **colored**

Ⓗ insert a comma after *is*

Ⓘ insert a period after *G*

17 What change should be made in sentence 8?

Ⓐ change *passes* to **pass**

Ⓑ change *such as* to **example**

Ⓒ change *drops of rain* to **raindrops**

Ⓓ change *of* to **for**

18 Which prepositional phrase could BEST be added to the end of sentence 10?

(F) in the same time

(G) at the same time

(H) of the same time

(I) with the same time

19 What change should be made in sentence 10?

(A) change *normal* to **normally**

(B) change *is raining* to **are raining**

(C) change *shining* to **shone**

(D) change the period to a question mark

20 What change should be made in sentence 11?

(F) change *sun* to **sun's**

(G) change *be* to **been**

(H) change *to* to **of**

(I) change the period to a question mark

Name _____ Date _____

Writing to Narrate

Read the prompt and plan your response.

> Most people have done something to help another person.
>
> Think about a time when you helped someone.
>
> Now write a story about a time when you helped someone.

Use this space to make your notes before you begin writing. The writing on this page will NOT be scored.

_____

_____

_____

_____

_____

_____

_____

Name _____ Date _____

Begin writing your response here. The writing on this page and the next page WILL be scored.

_____

_____

_____

_____

_____

_____

_____

_____

_____

_____

_____

_____

_____

_____

Name _____ Date _____

_____

_____

_____

_____

_____

_____

_____

_____

_____

_____

_____

_____

_____

_____

_____

_____

_____

_____

Reading Complex Text

Read the two passages "The First Fire: A Cherokee Legend" and "The Theft of Fire: A Sia Legend of New Mexico." As you read, stop and answer each question. Use evidence from the passages to support your answers.

The First Fire: A Cherokee Legend

from *Myths and Legends of the Great Plains,*
edited by Katharine Berry Judson

In the beginning there was no fire and the world was cold. Then the Thunders, who lived up in Galun'lati, sent their lightning and put fire into the bottom of a hollow sycamore tree, which grew on an island. The animals knew it was there because they could see the smoke coming out at the top, but they could not get to it on account of the water, so they held a council to decide what to do. This was a long, long time ago.

1 Describe the problem that the animals face.

_____

_____

_____

Every animal was anxious to go after the fire. Raven offered. He was large and strong, so he was sent first. He flew high and far across the water and lighted on the sycamore tree. There he perched, wondering what to do next. Then he looked at himself. The heat had scorched his feathers black. Raven was so frightened he flew back across the water without any fire.

Then little Wa-hu-hu, the Screech Owl, offered to go. He flew high and far across the water and perched upon a hollow tree. As he sat there looking into the hollow tree, wondering what to do, a blast of hot air came up and hurt his eyes. Screech Owl was frightened. He flew back as best he could, because he could hardly see. That is why his eyes are red even to this day.

Then Hooting Owl and the Horned Owl went, but by the time they reached the hollow tree, the fire was blazing so fiercely that the smoke nearly blinded them. The ashes carried up by the breeze made white rings around their eyes. So they had to come home without fire. Therefore they have white rings around their eyes.

None of the rest of the birds would go to the fire. Then Uk-su-hi, the racer snake, said he would go through the water and bring back fire. He swam to the island and crawled through the grass to the tree. Then he went into the tree by a small hole at the bottom. But the heat and smoke were dreadful. The ground at the bottom of the tree was covered with hot ashes. The racer darted back and forth trying to get off the ashes, and at last managed to escape through the same hole by which he had entered. But his body had been burned black. Therefore he is now the black racer. And that is why the black racer darts around and doubles on his track as if trying to escape.

Then great Blacksnake, "The Climber," offered to go for fire. He was much larger than the black racer. Blacksnake swam over to the island and climbed up the tree on the outside, as the blacksnake always does, but when he put his head down into the hole, the smoke choked him so that he fell into the burning stump. Before he could climb out, he, too, was burned black.

> ❷ According to the legend, what happened to make Blacksnake turn black?
>
> _____
>
> _____
>
> _____

So the birds, and the animals, and the snakes held another council. The world was still very cold. There was no fire. But all the birds, and the snakes, and all the four-footed animals refused to go for fire. They were all afraid of the burning sycamore.

Then Water Spider said she would go. This is not the water spider that looks like a mosquito, but the other one—the one with black downy hair and red stripes on her body. She could run on top of the water, or dive to the bottom.

The animals said, "How can you bring back fire?"

But Water Spider spun a thread from her body and wove it into a *tusti* bowl which she fastened on her back. Then she swam over to the island and through the grass to the fire. Water Spider put one little coal of fire into her bowl, and then swam back with it.

That is how fire came to the world. And that is why Water Spider has a *tusti* bowl on her back.

The Theft of Fire: A Sia Legend of New Mexico

from *Myths and Legends of California and the Old Southwest*, edited by Katharine Berry Judson

A long, long time ago, the people became tired of feeding on grass, like deer and wild animals, and they talked together how fire might be found. The Ti-amoni said, "Coyote is the best man to steal fire from the world below," so he sent for Coyote.

When Coyote came, the Ti-amoni said, "The people wish for fire . . . You must go to the world below and bring the fire."

Coyote said, "It is well, father—I will go."

So Coyote slipped stealthily to the house of Sussistinnako. It was the middle of the night. Snake, who guarded the first door, was asleep, and Coyote slipped quickly and quietly by. Cougar, who guarded the second door, was asleep, and Coyote slipped by. Bear, who guarded the third door, was also sleeping. . . . Slipping through into the room of Sussistinnako, Coyote found him also sleeping. Coyote quickly lighted the cedar brand, which was attached to his tail, and hurried out.

---

3 How does the point of view in "The First Fire" compare to the point of view in "The Theft of Fire"?

_____

_____

_____

Spider awoke, just enough to know someone was leaving the room. "Who is there?" he cried. Then he called, "Someone has been here." But before he could awaken the sleeping Bear and Cougar and Snake, Coyote had almost reached the upper world.

4 How is the challenge that the animals face in BOTH passages similar?

_____

_____

_____

_____

_____

Reading and Analyzing Text

Read the passages "Lost Pet" and "Trusting Experience" before answering Numbers 1 through 7.

Lost Pet

"Ziggy!" Jasmine stood on the porch and called her cat, but no orange-and-white tabby strolled out from behind the shrubs or from under the minivan in the driveway.

"Ziggy, where are you hiding?"

Searching inside the house had proved fruitless, so Jasmine returned to the yard, calling and calling her cat as she combed every hiding place she could remember. Ziggy had never been missing for so long before. Worried, Jasmine decided to ask her parents for help.

She found her mother in the den. "Mom, have you seen Ziggy?" she asked.

"Not since early this morning," her mother replied.

Next, Jasmine asked her father.

"I saw Ziggy strolling through the flowerbed, but that was hours ago," he said.

By now, Jasmine was sure Ziggy had gotten lost. It was time to take action, so she took a sheet of paper, sketched a picture of Ziggy, and then wrote "Lost Cat" and her phone number below the drawing. She included a detailed description of her cat: large orange tabby, golden eyes, and fluffy coat of fur. Jasmine photocopied the posters and asked her mother to help her hang them up around the neighborhood. Then they went home to wait for a call.

Within two hours, the phone rang. A friendly voice said, "My name is Mrs. Garcia, and I believe I have Ziggy. A huge orange tabby just strolled into my yard this afternoon. He has been resting on the porch, and he looks very comfortable."

"I'll be right over to see if it's Ziggy," Jasmine exclaimed after jotting down Mrs. Garcia's address.

Once Jasmine and her parents got to Mrs. Garcia's house, they discovered that the tabby was indeed Jasmine's lost Ziggy. Jasmine immediately scooped him up in her arms, nuzzled him, and buried her face in the soft fur of his neck. Ziggy closed his eyes and purred, as if his wandering away and being found again had been the most natural thing in the world.

Name _____ Date _____

Jasmine's parents thanked Mrs. Garcia for her help and drove their daughter and her beloved pet back home.

The next afternoon, Jasmine spotted Mrs. Garcia walking down the street, a worried expression on her face.

Jasmine waved to her and walked over. "Is something wrong?" she asked.

"Yes, Jasmine. It's odd, coming so soon after your adventure with Ziggy, but today my dog, Diego, is missing."

Mrs. Garcia described Diego's looks and personality.

"Is he a beagle?" Jasmine asked, and Mrs. Garcia nodded yes.

"I can help," Jasmine said. "I'll make posters for you and put them up."

Jasmine went home and hurriedly sketched a picture of a beagle. She added Mrs. Garcia's phone number, Diego's name and description, and some details about how he got lost. Again she made photocopies, and again her mother helped her hang them up.

That evening, Mrs. Garcia called Jasmine with the happy report that someone had identified a lost beagle in his neighborhood as Diego.

"You used your experience with Ziggy to help me," said Mrs. Garcia. "I really appreciate it. I'd like to invite you and your parents over tomorrow to meet Diego and to have some cookies," she continued.

"I look forward to it," Jasmine replied. "I'm so happy that both of our stories had happy endings!"

Trusting Experience

The wind screamed through the trees, vocalizing how I felt inside. The dogs dropped their chins and strained forward against the icy blasts of wind and snow that crisscrossed in front of us. As soon as I understood how dangerous this storm had become, I had turned the sled around toward home. Still, the trail had been made nearly invisible with snow. I made a kissing sound with my mouth and shouted, "Mush!" to my dog team. The wind stole my voice, but the dogs didn't need to hear to know that they needed to push ahead and continue to seek out the trail that would lead us home.

They were experienced sled dogs. They could sense the changing weather and the dangers that came with it. It was me who was the inexperienced one. That fact, which I had boldly disregarded earlier, was clear now. Suddenly, my lead dog Paq halted in his tracks. The six other dogs stopped, too. My heart sank as Paq looked earnestly back at me over his shoulder. It was as if he was trying to say, "I tried, but I cannot find the way." We had lost the trail. And my stubborn need to prove myself was to blame.

My thoughts drifted to the scene that had taken place that afternoon in my father's blacksmith shop. "Papa, I can handle the team. Uncle is counting on receiving that set of tools. Please, Papa! I've been on the Innoko Trail with you dozens of times," I begged.

"Miska, it's not that I don't trust you. Reports from the village are warning of an early fall storm. It doesn't matter how many times you have traveled that trail. You know how an Alaskan storm will blot out the trail before you can even say, 'Whoa,'" Papa responded, taking my chin in his rough, warm hand.

I shook his hand away in frustration. He probably planned to ask Yutu, the 17-year-old boy from the village who frequently ran Papa's dogsled team, to carry the tools to my uncle. I knew I could mush, or drive, just as well as Yutu. Although the air was biting cold, the sky above was cloudless. Surely I could outrace a storm that wasn't even on the horizon yet.

I left the shop in a huff and went directly to the kennel where our family kept our team of sled dogs. As I approached, several of the huskies rose to their feet. They wagged their tails in greeting. We loved and cared for our dogs like pets. First and foremost, however, our dogs were sled dogs. Their first love was mushing, carrying tools and supplies from my father's blacksmith shop to villages throughout the rural Alaskan valley. Even as Paq now sniffed the air cautiously, perhaps sensing the impending weather change, he would eagerly run

Name _____ Date _____

if given the command. In no time, I had harnessed the dogs. I stuffed the tools for my uncle along with food and blankets into the sled bag, and called, "Mush!" I did not look back.

Now, as the storm raged around my dogs and me, I knew the dangers that lay ahead if we couldn't recover the trail. Bracing myself against the wind, I left the sled and went to Paq at the lead. I took his large, snow-crusted head in my mittens, pleading with his warm brown eyes. "I'm so sorry, Paq. I should have listened to Papa. Now, I am relying on you. You must find that trail, Paq!" As if he understood my words, Paq lifted his head and sniffed the air. He whined, turning left and right, and buried his nose in the snow. Finally, his ears perked. His muscles stiffened. He had found the trail!

I darted back to the sled and picked up the tug lines. I would put all of my trust and faith in the experience and instinct of my lead dog, Paq. I closed my eyes and imagined our warm cabin and my father's worried eyes. I imagined how I would hug him tightly and tell him that I was sorry. "Take us home, Paq," I whispered.

Now answer Numbers 1 through 7. Base your answers on the passages "Lost Pet" and "Trusting Experience."

❶ Read this sentence from the passage "Lost Pet."

> **Searching inside the house had proved fruitless, so Jasmine returned to the yard, calling and calling her cat as she combed every hiding place she could remember.**

What does the phrase *combed every hiding place* mean in the sentence above?

Ⓐ gave thought to

Ⓑ went quickly to a place

Ⓒ imagined in one's mind

Ⓓ looked through carefully

Name _____ Date _____

2 What is the setting at the beginning of the passage "Lost Pet"?

ⓒ in Jasmine's yard and around her house

ⓓ on the front porch of Mrs. Garcia's house

ⓔ inside Jasmine's family's minivan while the family is driving

Ⓢ on the street in Jasmine's neighborhood where Jasmine is walking

3 Read this sentence from the passage "Trusting Experience."

The wind screamed through the trees, vocalizing how I felt inside.

Why does the author compare the wind to a person screaming in the sentence above?

Ⓐ to imply that the storm will soon pass

Ⓑ to suggest that the narrator is feeling angry

Ⓒ to show how intense and violent the storm is

Ⓓ to show how low the temperature has dropped

4 Which detail from the passage "Trusting Experience" BEST shows that inexperience can be dangerous in some situations?

ⓒ "Suddenly, my lead dog Paq halted in his tracks."

ⓓ "I made a kissing sound with my mouth and shouted, 'Mush!' to my dog team."

ⓔ "We had lost the trail. And my stubborn need to prove myself was to blame."

Ⓢ "The dogs dropped their chins and strained forward against the icy blasts of wind…"

5 Read this sentence from the passage "Trusting Experience."

I darted back to the sled and picked up the tug lines.

Why does the author use the word *darted* instead of *went* in the sentence above?

Ⓐ to show the narrator's fear of getting back on the sled

Ⓑ to show that the narrator does not move in a hurried way

Ⓒ to show how quickly the narrator moves back to the sled

Ⓓ to show how the narrator must walk carefully through the snow

6 Who narrates the passages "Lost Pet" and "Trusting Experience"?

Ⓕ Both passages are told from the author's point of view.

Ⓖ Both passages are told from the point of view of a young girl.

Ⓗ "Lost Pet" is told from the author's point of view, while "Trusting Experience" is told from the point of view of a young girl.

Ⓘ "Lost Pet" is told from the point of view of a young girl. while "Trusting Experience" is told from the author's point of view.

7 How are the lessons that Jasmine and Miska learn DIFFERENT?

Ⓐ Jasmine learns that new experiences can be scary. Miska learns that new experiences can be fun.

Ⓑ Jasmine learns that her own experiences can help her understand others. Miska learns that some experiences cannot be shared.

Ⓒ Jasmine learns that more experience will help her be a better pet owner. Miska learns that even experienced people make mistakes.

Ⓓ Jasmine learns that she can use her experience to help others. Miska learns that she must trust those who have more experience than her.

Read the article "Recycling" before answering Numbers 8 through 14.

Recycling

Have you ever used an old bag or box? If so, you have recycled. One way to recycle is to reuse old things in new ways. For example, you can make a desk organizer out of an egg carton, use the Sunday comics to wrap a present, or jot notes on the back of an old envelope.

Many cities recycle. Residents put the trash that can be recycled into special bins. Glass, plastic, newspaper, some metals, and sometimes foam are among the materials that are recycled. The bins are put out with the trash. Next, they are picked up by sanitation workers. Then, they are sorted and taken to processing plants and factories to make new products. Therefore, recycling means less garbage.

What becomes of our recycled objects? Many new products are made from old ones. For example, old foam is shredded and pressed together into a jumble of many-colored foam. The new foam is stuffed into pillows or used as carpet padding. Old paper turns up on store shelves as paper towels, cardboard, pet beds, and even as copier paper. Glass bottles and jars may be crushed into tiny pieces and used to pave roads. Or, they may be ground up into sand-size particles that are used on golf courses.

Recycled plastic has many uses. It is used to make toys, pens, pencils, fences, flowerpots, and outdoor furniture. Some kinds of plastic are even used to make soft, warm clothes!

It is important to recycle. It helps us to have less garbage. It also keeps us from wasting the Earth's trees and metals. When we recycle, we are being smart and taking care of the Earth, ourselves, and our future.

Look at the graph to see how many tons of paper each city recycles in a year.

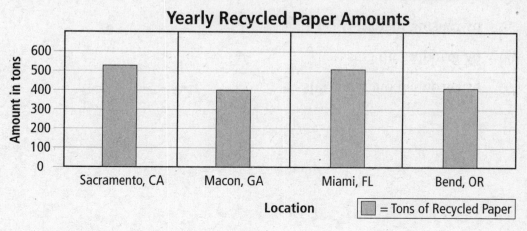

Yearly Recycled Paper Amounts

Name _____ Date _____

Now answer Numbers 8 through 14. Base your answers on the article "Recycling."

8 Read this sentence from the article.

> For example, old foam is shredded and pressed together into a jumble of many-colored foam.

What does the word *jumble* mean in the sentence above?

- Ⓕ mixture
- Ⓖ order
- Ⓗ pattern
- Ⓘ picture

9 Which detail from the article BEST supports the author's point that it is important to recycle?

- Ⓐ "Have you ever used an old bag or box?"
- Ⓑ "Residents put the trash that can be recycled into special bins."
- Ⓒ "The new foam is stuffed into pillows or used as carpet padding."
- Ⓓ "It helps us to have less garbage."

10 According to the article, what is one way people can reduce garbage in their homes?

- Ⓕ by crushing up jars
- Ⓖ by reusing materials
- Ⓗ by grinding up glass
- Ⓘ by throwing out materials

11 What will be the MAIN problem if people choose NOT to recycle?

Ⓐ No new products will be developed.

Ⓑ The earth's trees and metals will be wasted.

Ⓒ Cities will have to distribute more recycle bins.

Ⓓ Cities will have to hire more sanitation workers.

12 Which detail from the article BEST supports the fact that cities that recycle produce less garbage?

Ⓕ Recycled plastic can be used to make clothes.

Ⓖ Recycling is about taking care of the Earth and our future.

Ⓗ A recycled egg carton can be turned into a desk organizer.

Ⓘ Recycled materials are taken to factories to make new products.

13 How does the information in the graph BEST support the ideas in the article?

Ⓐ It shows how much paper certain U.S. cities recycle in a year.

Ⓑ It shows how much garbage certain cities throw away every year.

Ⓒ It shows how much money certain cities save by recycling paper.

Ⓓ It shows different products that can be made out of recycled paper.

14 Based on the information in the graph, what new products were MOST LIKELY made from the material that the four cities recycled?

Ⓕ road-paving materials

Ⓖ foam and carpet padding

Ⓗ cardboard and copier paper

Ⓘ flowerpots and outdoor furniture

Read the poem "The Library" before answering Numbers 15 through 20.

The Library

by Barbara A. Huff

It looks like any building
When you pass it on the street,
Made of stone and glass and marble,
Made of iron and concrete.

But once inside you can ride
A camel or a train,
Visit Rome, Siam, or Nome,
Feel a hurricane,
Meet a king, learn to sing,
How to bake a pie,
Go to sea, plant a tree,
Find how airplanes fly,
Train a horse, and of course
Have all the dogs you'd like,
See the moon, a sandy dune,
Or catch a whopping pike[1].
Everything that books can bring
You'll find inside those walls.
A world is there for you to share
When adventure calls.

You cannot tell its magic
By the way the building looks,
But there's wonderment within it,
The wonderment of books.

[1] **pike:** a freshwater fish

Now answer Numbers 15 through 20. Base your answers on the poem "The Library."

15 According to the author, what does the library look like when FIRST passed on the street?

Ⓐ a foreign city

Ⓑ a magical place

Ⓒ a regular building

Ⓓ a place near the sea

16 Read these lines from the poem.

> **But once inside you can ride
> A camel or a train,**

What does the author mean in the lines above?

Ⓕ You can pet a camel.

Ⓖ You can buy a train ticket.

Ⓗ You can find libraries near train tracks.

Ⓘ You can read books about camels or trains.

17 What does the author compare the library to in this poem?

Ⓐ cities

Ⓑ people

Ⓒ storms

Ⓓ other buildings

18 Read these lines from the poem.

> **A world is there for you to share
> When adventure calls.**

What does the author mean by the phrase *when adventure calls* in the
lines above?

- Ⓕ when an experience is unexpected
- Ⓖ when a traveling experience comes to an end
- Ⓗ when an exciting experience is wanted or needed
- Ⓘ when an experience seems exciting but really isn't

19 What is the theme of this poem?

- Ⓐ Libraries often hold special events and activities.
- Ⓑ Reading books is the best way to gain knowledge.
- Ⓒ Everyone should travel at some point in their lives.
- Ⓓ Reading can introduce you to new ideas and experiences.

20 Based on how the author describes the library, what does the reader know about
the author?

- Ⓕ She likes to eat.
- Ⓖ She likes to read.
- Ⓗ She likes to cook.
- Ⓘ She likes to garden.

Read the article "Journaling" before answering Numbers 21 through 25.

Journaling

The word *journal* sounds a lot like the word *journey*—for a good reason. Both words come from a French word meaning "day's work." When you journal, you keep a record of your journey through life, often one day at a time. A journal can be a place where you write down your feelings and your memories of events: You can use a journal to record your observations about the world around you or interesting facts you have learned. You can even make up stories and poems and write them in your journal!

There are many advantages to writing in a journal. First, journaling can make you feel better. Sometimes, we just need a place to let off steam and express feelings we might otherwise keep cooped up inside. Secondly, journaling makes you think deeply. Reflecting on feelings and experiences is important for learning and improving oneself. Journaling can help you become a better writer. Writing and communication skills are important in so many areas of life—from school, to a future job, to your relationships with people. Journaling gives you lots of writing practice. The journaling process is pretty straightforward, but like anything, it can take practice and getting into a routine.

So, how do you go about starting and keeping a journal?

1 The first thing you need is an actual space in which to record your thoughts. In other words, you need blank pages! You can buy a book with blank pages. You can also easily make a book out of plain, white paper. If you prefer to type, you can create a journal on a computer.

2 Next, you will need to set aside some time for yourself to write. This is the hardest part about beginning a journal: finding a routine and sticking to it. Maybe you will decide to journal every morning before school, or maybe every other night before bed. Treat your journal like a good friend; make time for it.

3 Have a quiet place where you can go and write. It can be hard to think, reflect, and write when you are in a noisy place.

4 Have fun with your journal! Try out different types of writing. Reflect on a concept you learned about in science. Test out your poetry-writing skills. Recall a favorite childhood memory.

5 Every once in a while, flip back through the pages of your journal and read what you have written. You might laugh at a funny memory or remember an interesting thing you witnessed on a hike. Best of all, you can see what you've learned, how you've grown, and where you've journeyed to and from!

Happy journaling!

Now answer Numbers 21 through 25. Base your answers on the article "Journaling."

21 Read this sentence from the article.

> **The journaling process is pretty straightforward, but like anything, it can take practice getting into a routine.**

What does the word *straightforward* mean in the sentence above?

Ⓐ easy

Ⓑ meaningful

Ⓒ strange

Ⓓ vague

22 Read this sentence from the article "Journaling."

> **Treat your journal like a good friend; make time for it.**

Why does the author compare a journal to a good friend in the sentence above?

Ⓕ to show that a journal should be hidden in a safe place

Ⓖ to show how similar journaling and talking to friends are

Ⓗ to show how important it is to dedicate oneself to journal-writing

Ⓘ to show that a journal is something that needs to be shared with others

Name _____ Date _____

23 Read this sentence from the article.

Recall a favorite childhood memory.

What does the word *recall* mean in the sentence above?

Ⓐ become unfamiliar

Ⓑ remove or take away

Ⓒ receive from someone

Ⓓ bring back into one's mind

24 Which detail from the article BEST supports the idea that there are many advantages to writing in a journal?

Ⓕ "The word *journal* sounds a lot like the word *journey*—for a good reason."

Ⓖ "Reflecting on feelings and experiences is important for learning and improving oneself."

Ⓗ "The first thing you need is an actual space in which to record your thoughts."

Ⓘ "If you prefer to type, you can create a journal on your computer."

25 Which sentence BEST describes how the end of the article is organized?

Ⓐ It compares drawing with writing in a journal.

Ⓑ It tells the steps in order to start and keep a journal.

Ⓒ It describes what a journal is and how they are used.

Ⓓ It proves the importance of using a journal in school.

Read the passage "Gathering Food" before answering Numbers 26 through 30.

Gathering Food

From the moment Adahy caught a glimpse of the big orange sun appearing over the mountain tops, he was positive that today would be a great day. Adahy and his friends would gather acorns to store for the winter months. This was an important task because the acorns would nourish the people in the cave when food was scarce.

Adahy anticipated his friends emerging from the cave, and then the three of them would start searching for acorns. Adahy stared at the giant oak and hickory trees that surrounded the cave. He contemplated the various tasks assigned to each person who lived in the cave. The men built tools for hunting and fishing. The women made pots and gathered berries, roots, and seeds to eat during winter.

Finally, Tooantuh and Sheasequat appeared. Sheasequat glanced at Adahy's empty hands. He asked, "Adahy, do you have a pot to put the acorns in?"

"Oh, I forgot, but I will get it now," said Adahy. He disappeared into the cave and quickly returned with two large clay pots.

Adahy, Tooantuh, and Sheasequat started out on the path into the forest. The trees towered over the boys, forming a tunnel into the woods. The boys were cautious about staying together and on the path. They listened closely to the sounds of the forest. They strained their ears to hear squirrels chattering. That was a telltale sign of nearby acorns.

"Stop!" Tooantuh whispered, holding out his hand. "I think I hear them." The boys halted. They looked up and spotted several squirrels scampering among the trees.

"There they are," Sheasequat said. "Now we are sure to find what we need."

As squirrels scurried over their heads, Sheasequat, Tooantuh, and Adahy searched for acorns. They explored the forest around them and uncovered acorns under dried leaves and twigs. The squirrels found the acorns, too, in the oak branches above. Together the boys and the squirrels collected

Name _____ Date _____

food for the winter. The squirrels would hoard them in their nests, while the people of the cave would store them in dirt holes to cool and preserve them.

When their pots were bursting with acorns, the boys returned to the path that would take them back to the cave. They would present the overflowing pots to Adsila, the food keeper, when they arrived.

"Adsila," they called proudly as they entered the cave. "Look what we have found."

Adsila turned to the boys and smiled. "You have done a great job. These acorns will feed many of us when it begins to snow. See what the women have collected for us." She gestured toward the holes in the cave floor.

Adahy and his friends peered into one of the holes in the dirt. They saw seeds, roots, and nuts. The boys' pots of acorns made a significant contribution to the stores of winter food and would require a new hole. This winter, no one in the cave would go hungry.

Adahy was full of pride. He and his friends were helping to feed the cave families. He strolled out the cave entrance and gazed at the yellow sun setting behind the mountain tops against the rosy sky. Tomorrow would be an excellent day to forage for more food with Sheasequat and Tooantuh.

Now answer Numbers 26 through 30. Base your answers on the passage "Gathering Food."

26 Where does MOST of this passage take place?

   F   in a tree

   G   in a cave

   H   on a path

   I   near a stream

27 What problem does Adahy face BEFORE he gathers acorns?

- Ⓐ His friends disappear.
- Ⓑ He forgets his clay pots.
- Ⓒ His friends refuse to help.
- Ⓓ He forgets his fishing tool.

28 Read the sentence from the passage.

> **The squirrels would hoard them in their nests, while the people of the cave would store them in dirt holes to cool and preserve them.**

What does the word *preserve* mean in the sentence above?

- Ⓕ allow to harden
- Ⓖ ground into pieces
- Ⓗ keep from spoiling
- Ⓘ get ready for a special occasion

29 Which word BEST describes Adahy and the cave families?

- Ⓐ forgetful
- Ⓑ hard-working
- Ⓒ lazy
- Ⓓ over-confident

30 What is the theme of the passage?

- Ⓕ Working together pays off in the end.
- Ⓖ Walking in nature results in happiness.
- Ⓗ Enjoying the simple things in life is important.
- Ⓘ Caring for the environment makes the world a better place.

Name _____ Date _____

Read the article "Fly High, Bessie Coleman" before answering Numbers 31 through 35.

Fly High, Bessie Coleman

by Jane Sutcliffe

Two thousand people sat with their faces turned to the sky. High above the airfield, a pilot had just finished carving a crisp figure eight in the air. Suddenly, the plane seemed to stumble. Twisting and turning, it began to fall from the sky. The crowd watched in horror. Had something happened to the pilot?

But the woman in the cockpit of the plane on October 15, 1922, was in perfect control. Only two hundred feet above the ground she straightened out the tumbling aircraft and soared back into the sky. By the time she landed her plane, the crowd was on its feet, roaring with delight. Everyone cheered for Bessie Coleman, the first licensed black pilot in the world.

Coleman, in uniform, stands on the runner of a Model T Ford. The nose and right wing of her plane are to her left.

Growing Up

Bessie Coleman was born on January 26, 1892. She was a bright girl and a
star pupil in school. In Waxahachie, Texas, where Bessie grew up, black children
and white children attended different schools. Each year Bessie's school closed
for months at a time. Instead of studying, the children joined their parents
picking cotton on big plantations. Bessie's mother was proud of her daughter's
sharp mind. She didn't want Bessie to spend her life picking cotton, and urged
her to do something special with her life.

Learning to Fly

In 1915, when she was 23, Bessie Coleman moved to Chicago. She found
a job as a manicurist in a men's barbershop. Coleman loved her job and the
interesting people she met there. After the United States entered World War I
in 1917, soldiers returning from the war often came to the shop. Coleman was
fascinated by their stories of daredevil pilots. She read everything she could
about airplanes and flying. She later recalled, "All the articles I read finally
convinced me I should be up there flying and not just reading about it."

Bessie Coleman asked some of Chicago's pilots for lessons. They refused. No
one thought that an African American woman could learn to fly.

In desperation, Coleman asked Robert Abbott for help. Abbott owned
Chicago's African American newspaper, *The Chicago Defender*. He had often
promised to help members of the black community with their problems. Abbott
told Coleman to forget about learning to fly in the United States. Go to France,
he said to her, where no one would care if her skin was black or white.

So she did. First Coleman learned to speak French. Then she applied to a
French flying school and was accepted. On November 20, 1920, Coleman sailed
for France, where she spent the next seven months taking flying lessons. She
learned to fly straight and level, and to turn and bank the plane. She practiced
making perfect landings. On a second trip to Europe, she spent months mastering
rolls, loops, and spins. These were the tricks she would need if she planned to
make her living as a performing pilot.

Performing in Airshows

Coleman returned to the United States in the summer of 1922. Wherever
she performed, other African Americans wanted to know where they, too, could
learn to fly. It was a question that made Coleman sad. She hoped that she could
make enough money from her airshows to buy her own plane. Then she could
open a school so everyone would have a chance to feel the freedom she felt in the
sky.

By early 1923, Coleman was close to her goal. She had saved her money and bought a plane. Then, as she was flying to an airshow in California, her engine stalled. The brand-new plane crashed to the ground.

Coleman suffered a broken leg and three broken ribs. Still, she refused to quit. "Tell them all that as soon as I can walk I'm going to fly!" she wrote to friends and fans.

Coleman's pilot license was issued on June 15, 1921, in France. The year of her birth is incorrect. Bessie Coleman was born in 1892, not 1896.

Many people, both black and white, were very impressed by Coleman's determination. A white businessman helped her buy another plane. By 1926, Coleman was back where she had been before the crash. She wrote to her sister, "I am right on the threshold of opening a school."

In 1929, three years after her death, the Bessie Coleman Aero Clubs were formed. The clubs encouraged and trained African American pilots—just as Coleman had hoped to do. In 1931, the clubs sponsored the first All-African-American airshow. Bessie Coleman would have been proud.

Name _____ Date _____

Now answer Numbers 31 through 35. Base your answers on the article "Fly High, Bessie Coleman."

31 Read this sentence from the article.

> **By the time she landed her plane, the crowd was on its feet, roaring with delight.**

Which word means almost the SAME as the word *delight* in the sentence above?

- (A) creativity
- (B) fear
- (C) fury
- (D) pleasure

32 According to the author, what is one reason why Coleman FIRST became interested in becoming a pilot?

- (F) She had traveled to France where she had visited a pilot training school.
- (G) As a child, she had been told that African Americans could not learn to fly planes.
- (H) She was inspired by stories about daring World War I pilots from soldiers she met.
- (I) She did not enjoy working in a male barbershop and wanted to do something different.

33 Which detail BEST supports the author's opinion that Coleman would have been proud to see the first All-African-American airshow?

(A) It had been her goal to open a school to train African American pilots.

(B) Many of the students she had trained participated in the show as pilots.

(C) She had loved to watch others perform as much as she enjoyed performing herself.

(D) She was the one who formed the Bessie Coleman Aero Clubs, the group that sponsored the show.

34 How do the headings help the reader understand the information in the article?

(F) They help in recalling important dates in Coleman's life.

(G) They help in locating information about key events in Coleman's life.

(H) They help in picturing what it would have been like to watch Coleman fly.

(I) They help in identifying what pilots go through when they first learn to fly.

35 Which sentence BEST describes how the article is organized?

(A) It explains the important events of one person's life in order.

(B) It tells the steps one must take to become a famous pilot.

(C) It compares and contrasts flying with other daring performances.

(D) It explains the problems in learning to fly and how they are solved.

Revising and Editing

Read the introduction and the article "Jeanne Birdsall" before answering Numbers 1 through 6.

Wendy wrote this article about her favorite author. Read her article and think about the changes she should make.

Jeanne Birdsall

(1) Jeanne Birdsall is an award-winning children's author. (2) Birdsall says her sixth-grade teacher helped her develop creative thinking and writing skills.

(3) Her first book was The Penderwicks: A Summer Tale of Four Sisters, Two Rabbits, and a Very Interesting Boy. (4) Birdsall also wrote a sequel called The Penderwicks On Gardam Street. (5) In all, Birdsall plans to write a total of five books along the Penderwick family. (6) She says it takes her about three years to write one book.

(7) Birdsall bases her characters on real people and takes many ideas for her books from her life. (8) The Penderwicks are a really real family. (9) They are not perffect, and their problems could really happen to people. (10) Mr. Penderwick, the father, has four daughters.

(11) Rosalind is the oldest. (12) The other three daughters are Skye, Jane, and Batty. (13) The Penderwick children are a little bit like the children in Birdsall's family.

(14) Animals play a big part in Birdsall's life and they are important in her books, too. (15) Birdsall has many pets, including a dog named Cagney.

Name _____ Date _____

(16) She named her dog after a gardener named Cagney in her Penderwick books. (17) While writing her first book, Birdsall had pet rabbits named Jane and Horatio. (18) She based a character's pets, Carla and Yaz, on her rabbits.

Now answer Numbers 1 through 6. Base your answers on the changes Wendy should make.

1 Which sentence could BEST be added after sentence 1?

Ⓐ I read books by lots of other authors, too.

Ⓑ The people who illustrate books can also win awards.

Ⓒ She knew she wanted to be an author when she was only ten years old.

Ⓓ I enjoy writing stories and hope to write a novel when I become an adult.

2 What change should be made in sentence 4?

Ⓕ change *wrote* to **wroet**

Ⓖ insert a comma after *called*

Ⓗ change *On* to **on**

Ⓘ change the period to a question mark

3 What change should be made in sentence 5?

Ⓐ delete the comma after *all*

Ⓑ change *to* to **on**

Ⓒ change *books* to **book**

Ⓓ change *along* to **about**

4 What change should be made in sentence 8?

- Ⓕ change *are* to **is**

- Ⓖ change *a* to **an**

- Ⓗ change *really real* to **realistic**

- Ⓘ change the period to a comma

5 What change should be made in sentence 9?

- Ⓐ change *perffect* to **perfect**

- Ⓑ change *their* to **they're**

- Ⓒ change *to* to **for**

- Ⓓ change *people* to **peoples**

6 What change should be made in sentence 14?

- Ⓕ change *big* to **biggest**

- Ⓖ change *Birdsall's* to **Birdsalls**

- Ⓗ insert a *comma* after **life**

- Ⓘ insert *also* after **and**

**Read the introduction and the passage "A Balloon Ride" before answering
Numbers 7 through 12.**

*Andrew wrote this passage about a memorable event. Read his passage
and think about the changes he should make.*

A Balloon Ride

(1) Yesterday afternoon I went with my family to our town's annual

hot-air balloon festival. (2) When we arrived, the balloons were not

inflated. (3) Then, the pilots turned on the burners, and the balloons

started to inflate. (4) Within minutes, the pilots lifted the balloons off the

ground and transformed the sky into a polka-dot rainbow. (5) We watched

from the ground as the balloons got smaller and smaller.

(6) At this point, we would usual leave the festival, but on this day, my

uncle took my hand, and we strolled to a lone hot-air balloon. (7) I was

stunned when the pilot opened the basket door and told us to step inside.

(8) My mouth fell open, and I stared at the pilot in a days. (9) When my

uncle explained that he had bought tickets for us to ride in the balloon, I

couldn't believe my ears!

(10) Inside the basket, the pilot began by explaining the safety rules.

(11) He turned on the burner. (12) There was a loud whooshing sound as

a six-foot flame shot up into the balloon. (13) Eventually we lifted off the

pavemint and were soon soaring in the sky. (14) The pilot uses the heated air to control the movement of the balloon. (15) Neither my uncle nor I

could believe how smooth the ride was.

(16) During the ride, I asked the pilot a few questions, but I mainly just

enjoyed the peacefully ride. (17) Back on the ground, the pilot took our

picture to use in his advertisements. (18) What an exciting day.

Now answer Numbers 7 through 12. Base your answers on the changes Andrew should make.

7 What change should be made in sentence 6?

- Ⓐ change *usual* to **usually**
- Ⓑ change *leave* to **leeve**
- Ⓒ delete the comma after *festival*
- Ⓓ change *uncle* to **Uncle**

8 What change should be made in sentence 8?

- Ⓕ change *fell* to **fall**
- Ⓖ change *and* to **but**
- Ⓗ change *the pilot* to **he**
- Ⓘ change *days* to **daze**

9 What change should be made in sentence 13?

- Ⓐ change *lifted* to **lift**
- Ⓑ change *off* to **of**
- Ⓒ change *pavemint* to **pavement**
- Ⓓ insert a comma after *soaring*

Name _____ Date _____

10 What change should be made in sentence 14?

- Ⓕ change *uses* to **used**

- Ⓖ change *to* to **too**

- Ⓗ change *movement* to **movment**

- Ⓘ change *of* to **above**

11 What change should be made in sentence 16?

- Ⓐ insert a comma after *During*

- Ⓑ change *asked* to **ask**

- Ⓒ insert a period after *questions*

- Ⓓ change *peacefully* to **peaceful**

12 What change should be made in sentence 18?

- Ⓕ insert a comma after *What*

- Ⓖ change *an* to **a**

- Ⓗ change *exciting* to **excited**

- Ⓘ change the period to an exclamation point

Read the introduction and the article "The Constitution" before answering Numbers 13 through 19.

Marcel wrote this article about the Constitution. Read his article and think about the changes he should make.

The Constitution

(1) More than 200 years ago, a group of men came together to write the Constitution of the United States of america. (2) This document described how the United States government would work. (3) It may be the importantest document in the history of the United States. (4) It has governed the people of the United States since 1789.

(5) The authors of the Constitution knew that it might be necessary to change the document so they decided on the exact steps for how it could be changed. (6) In 1791, the first of these changes, called amendments, were added to the Constitution. (7) These first ten amendments. (8) Are called the Bill of Rights. (9) They protect the rights of the people of the United States. (10) The First Amendment gives people the freedom to follow any religion, or none at all. (11) It also protects freedom of speech, freedom of the press, and the right of people to gather together.

(12) Over the years, other amendments have been added to the Constitution. (13) In 1865, the Thirteenth Amendment ended slavery. (14) We studied the end of slavery in school. (15) In 1920, the Nineteenth Amendment gived women the right to vote. (16) Changes have also been made in recent

times. (17) In 1992, the Twenty-Seventh Amendment was added. (18) It states that lawmakers cannot raise their pay while still in office.

(19) In the future, more changes will likely need to be made to the Constitution. (20) Amendments will be suggested and lawmakers will vote on them. (21) If most lawmakers agree with a change. (22) It will become part of the Constitution.

Now answer Numbers 13 through 19. Base your answers on the changes Marcel should make.

13 What change should be made in sentence 1?

Ⓐ delete the comma after *ago*

Ⓑ change *group* to **groop**

Ⓒ insert a period after *together*

Ⓓ change *america* to **America**

14 What change should be made in sentence 3?

Ⓕ change *be* to **been**

Ⓖ change *importantest* to **most important**

Ⓗ insert a comma after *document*

Ⓘ change *history* to **historey**

15 What change should be made in sentence 5?

Ⓐ insert a comma after *Constitution*

Ⓑ change *knew* to **know**

Ⓒ insert a comma after *document*

Ⓓ change *exact* to **exactly**

16 What revision is needed in sentences 7 and 8?

Ⓕ These first ten amendments are called the Bill of Rights.

Ⓖ These first ten amendments are called. The Bill of Rights.

Ⓗ These first ten amendments, are called The Bill of Rights.

Ⓘ These first ten amendments and are called the Bill of Rights.

17 What change should be made in sentence 15?

Ⓐ delete the comma after *1920*

Ⓑ change *gived* to **gave**

Ⓒ change *women* to **womin**

Ⓓ change *vote* to **voted**

18 What is the BEST way to rewrite sentences 21 and 22?

Ⓕ If most lawmakers agree with a change, it will become part of the Constitution.

Ⓖ If most lawmakers, agree with a change, so it will become part of the Constitution.

Ⓗ If most lawmakers agree. With a change, it will become part of the Constitution.

Ⓘ If most lawmakers agree, and a change will become part of the Constitution.

19 Which sentence does NOT belong in this article?

Ⓐ sentence 6

Ⓑ sentence 11

Ⓒ sentence 14

Ⓓ sentence 18

Read the introduction and the passage "The Spelling Bee" before answering Numbers 20 through 25.

Hannah wrote this passage about a boy who enters a spelling bee. Read her passage and think about the changes she should make.

The Spelling Bee

(1) Robert always made very, really good grades on his spelling tests. (2) His teacher, Mr. McNeil, challenged Robert to enter the school spelling bee, and he accepted. (3) Robert thought winning the spelling bee would be effortless.

(4) Mr. McNeil gave Robert a list of words to study to help him get ready about the spelling bee. (5) When Robert scanned the list, he was suddenly not so sure of hisself. (6) The words were so difficult he could not even read none them. (7) Many of the words had 16 letters, more than half of all the letters in the alphabet. (8) Robert wondered if it was too late to withdraw from the competition. (9) However, he did not want to dissplease his teacher, so he decided to give it his best effort.

(10) Robert talked to his family about the spelling bee. (11) Everyone was excited about it, and said they would help him prepare. (12) His brother even promised to help him study every night. (13) For two weeks Robert practiced for at least one hour every day after school. (14) The words became easier to spell, and he made fewer guesses.

(15) Robert won the school spelling bee and entered the city spelling bee. (16) What do you think happened? (17) The answer appeared on the front page of the community newspaper. (18) The article's headline read, "Local Boy wins Second Place." (19) Now Robert is studying for next year's competition!

Now answer Numbers 20 through 25. Base your answers on the changes Hannah should make.

20 What change should be made in sentence 1?

Ⓕ change *very, really good* to **excellent**

Ⓖ change *grades* to **grade**

Ⓗ change *on* to **to**

Ⓘ change *the period* to **a question mark**

21 What change should be made in sentence 4?

Ⓐ change *Mr.* to **Mr**

Ⓑ change *gave* to **gived**

Ⓒ change *get* to **got**

Ⓓ change *about* to **for**

22 What change should be made in sentence 5?

Ⓕ change *When* to **So**

Ⓖ delete the comma after *list*

Ⓗ change *suddenly* to **sudden**

Ⓘ change *hisself* to **himself**

23 What change should be made in sentence 6?

Ⓐ insert a comma after *were*

Ⓑ change *could* to **couldn't**

Ⓒ change *none* to **some of**

Ⓓ change *them* to **the**

24 What change should be made in sentence 9?

Ⓕ change *did not* to **did'nt**

Ⓖ change *dissplease* to **displease**

Ⓗ delete the comma after *teacher*

Ⓘ change *effort* to **efort**

25 What change should be made in sentence 18?

Ⓐ change *article's* to **articles**

Ⓑ change *read* to **is reading**

Ⓒ change *wins* to **Wins**

Ⓓ insert a period after the final quotation mark

Writing to Inform

Read the prompt and plan your response.

> Many inventions have made our lives easier in one way
> or another.
>
> Think about an important invention that has made your
> life easier.
>
> Now write to explain how an invention has made your life easier.

**Use this space to make your notes before you begin writing. The writing on
this page will NOT be scored.**

_____

_____

_____

_____

_____

_____

_____

Name _____ Date _____

Begin writing your response here. The writing on this page and the next page WILL be scored.

_____

_____

_____

_____

_____

_____

_____

_____

_____

_____

_____

_____

_____

_____

_____

Name _____ Date _____

_____

_____

_____

_____

_____

_____

_____

_____

_____

_____

_____

_____

_____

_____

_____

_____

Reading Complex Text

Read the article "Mary Anderson and Florence Lawrence Pave the Way for Safer Automobiles." As you read, stop and answer each question. Use evidence from the article to support your answers.

Mary Anderson and Florence Lawrence Pave the Way for Safer Automobiles

The automobile has been a work in progress ever since its invention in the late 1800s. Today, all cars have windshield wipers, turn signals, and brake lights. However, the first cars had none of these features, because no one had invented them yet! Windshield wipers, turn signals, and stop signals (which were later replaced by brake lights) were the ideas of two forward-thinking women in the early 1900s. These two pioneers, Mary Anderson and Florence Lawrence, were the first to introduce these important features. Now, these features are standard in cars everywhere.

---

1 What does the word *pioneers* mean in this article?

_____

_____

_____

Mary Anderson came up with the idea of windshield wipers during a trip to New York City in 1903. An Alabama native, Anderson had never faced a winter in the "Big Apple" before. She was struck by how drivers dealt with the cold, wet conditions. As rain, ice, and snow fell, drivers could not see clearly through their windshields. Anderson saw drivers constantly stop to clean off their windshields. How easy it would be, she thought, if drivers could clear their windshields from inside the car! If only they could just flip a switch. She set to work. The switch, or lever, would connect to an arm. The arm, or wiper, would be covered by a rubber blade. All the driver had to do was press the switch inside the car. Ta da! The arm would swing across the windshield. As it did, it would clear away the rain, ice, and snow. In 1904, Anderson won a patent for her invention. Windshield wipers were born. Now, drivers could

Name _____ Date _____

easily clear their windshields from inside the car. This made driving safer and more convenient.

> **2** What problem did Mary Anderson recognize? What was her solution?
>
> _____
>
> _____
>
> _____

In the following decade, the automobile industry exploded. Thanks to advances in how cars were manufactured, they could now be mass-produced. In 1908, Henry Ford introduced his popular Model T. By 1913, these cars (each boasting a pair of mechanical windshield wipers) became more widely available and cheaper to buy. More and more Americans could now afford cars.

That same year, a New York City movie star named Florence Lawrence purchased her very own car. If there was anything Lawrence loved as much as acting, it was driving. More than that, she loved thinking about ways to improve cars. At that time, there was no built-in device that allowed drivers to signal a turn. This was a problem as drivers had to guess where and when other drivers planned to turn. A wrong guess could result in a serious accident. To fix this problem, Lawrence invented an "auto signaling arm." The arm was located on the back end, or rear, of the car. A set of buttons by the driver's seat triggered the arm. When the driver pressed a button, the arm would raise or lower a sign. The sign told which direction the driver intended to turn. This simple device allowed drivers to better communicate with each other on the road and avoid accidents.

> **3** How did Florence Lawrence's "auto signaling arm" work?
>
> _____
>
> _____
>
> _____

Name _____ Date _____

It seems awfully dangerous to think about driving without turn signals. Consider, too, that these early cars lacked any built-in "stop" signal. Drivers had no reliable way to signal to other drivers that they were using their brakes to slow down or stop. Lawrence developed a feature much like the turn signal. This signal enabled drivers to alert others of their plan to stop. How did it work? When drivers stepped on the brake pedal, a "stop" sign would pop up in the car's rear. Unlike Anderson, Lawrence never patented her inventions. Eventually, the stop signal was replaced by brake lights. Now, lights come on at the car's rear when a driver steps on the brakes. Unlike Lawrence's signal, other drivers can see a car's brake lights even in the dark.

The devices created by Anderson and Lawrence have certainly changed in the last 100 years. Modern cars now run on sophisticated electrical systems with onboard computers. These systems monitor and control nearly everything a car can do. Of course, this includes windshield wipers, turn signals, and brake lights. Like most great inventors, Anderson and Lawrence used their creative powers to solve problems. Their ideas made cars safer for all drivers. These two innovative women helped lay the groundwork for important features that are standard in cars today.

---

4 Discuss TWO ways that Mary Anderson's and Florence Lawrence's ideas impacted the automobile industry.

_____

_____

_____

_____

_____

Name _____ Date _____

Reading and Analyzing Text

Read the passage "At the Beach, at Last" before answering Numbers 1 through 18.

At the Beach, at Last

This passage is about a girl named Marina. Marina visited the beach last summer.

I've always wanted to visit the beach, and last summer I finally got to go. While there, I saw many people swimming, building sandcastles, and playing games. I did those things, too, but they are not what I enjoyed most. I got to focus on studying the wildlife that lives by the ocean, just like a marine biologist. A marine biologist is a scientist who studies living things that inhabit[1] the ocean. I first learned about these scientists last year on a third-grade field trip to the city aquarium. Ever since then, I've wanted to be a marine biologist when I grow up.

Before our beach trip, I reread my favorite book, Guide to the Seashore, which I bought at the aquarium bookstore. At home, I packed the book, along with my clothes, hats, towels, water shoes, and sunscreen. For my observations, I packed a spiral notebook, pencils, a camera, and a magnifying glass. I couldn't wait to explore the beach like a real marine biologist.

---

[1] **inhabit:** live in

Name _____ Date _____

Finally, it was time for our trip. My mother and I traveled by car with my aunt and my two cousins. After about six hours in the car, we arrived at the beach house we were renting for the week. Everyone was excited to get to the water, so we quickly put on our beach gear and sunscreen and walked down to the beach. I stood next to my mom and held her hand. The heavy air was unlike anything I had ever experienced. The wind carried the smell of salt water as it whipped my hair. I couldn't stop the smile that spread across my face. Finally, I was at the beach!

While my cousins and my aunt played in the sand, Mom and I started to explore. I found a tide pool with fish and other animals to inspect, so I pulled my book from my backpack and began flipping through the pages. I was able to identify two different kinds of fish and a sea urchin, too. I wanted to take the animals with me, but I knew I shouldn't disturb them. After a while, Mom and I walked back toward my aunt and cousins.

Suddenly, I heard splashing behind us. Mom and I turned around to see a boy, about twelve years old, jumping into the tide pool. I gave Mom a pleading look. She nodded, understanding, and we rushed back to the tide pool. "Stop!" I called.

The boy looked at me. "What?" he demanded. "I'm not hurting anything."

That's when I explained that he was, in fact, hurting something. He was disturbing the tide pool.

"The what?" he asked with a mixture of anger and confusion.

"You're jumping in a tide pool," I said. "The shallow water in a tide pool is actually home to many tiny living creatures. Just look."

The boy looked at his feet, shook his head, and mumbled, "Impossible." I encouraged him to look closer.

He bent down, placing his face near the water, and looked closely. "Wow!" he exclaimed. "There are things swimming in here."

"Yes, that's right," I said. "I have a book that explains all about the animals and their home. Do you want to learn about these tide pool creatures, too?"

"Wow, you bet!" he agreed. Then Mom, the boy, and I sat down next to the tide pool and opened the book. I pointed out what I'd learned just moments before.

"Wow, you know a lot about marine animals."

"That's because I want to be a marine biologist," I said with confidence.

Another awe-inspired, "Wow," was all he could manage to say.

Name _____ Date _____

Now answer Numbers 1 through 18. Base your answers on the passage "At the Beach, at Last."

1 Where does MOST of this passage take place?

Ⓐ at a beach

Ⓑ at a school

Ⓒ at a bookstore

Ⓓ at an aquarium

2 Read this sentence from the passage.

While there, I saw many people swimming, building sandcastles, and playing games.

Which consonant is silent in the word *sandcastles*?

Ⓕ n

Ⓖ c

Ⓗ t

Ⓘ l

3 Read this sentence from the passage.

I got to focus on studying the wildlife that lives by the ocean, just like a marine biologist.

What does the word *focus* mean in the sentence above?

Ⓐ create

Ⓑ concentrate

Ⓒ ignore

Ⓓ remember

4 Read the dictionary entry below.

> a•quar•i•um \ə-kwâr'-ē-əm\ *noun* **1.** a tank or bowl for living fish and plants. **2.** A place for the public display of wild animals and plants in water [from Latin *aquārium*, source of water]

What is the origin of the word *aquarium*?

- Ⓕ display
- Ⓖ fish
- Ⓗ Latin
- Ⓘ public

5 What made Marina decide to become a marine biologist?

- Ⓐ a vacation at the beach
- Ⓑ a book about the beach
- Ⓒ the animals in a tide pool
- Ⓓ a visit to the city aquarium

6 Read this sentence from the passage.

> **For my observations, I packed a spiral notebook, pencils, a camera, and a magnifying glass.**

What is the CORRECT way to stress the syllables in the word *observations*?

- Ⓕ OB • ser • va • tions
- Ⓖ ob • ser • va • TIONS
- Ⓗ ob • SER • va • tions
- Ⓘ ob • ser • VA • tions

Name _____ Date _____

7 Read this sentence from the passage.

> **For my observations, I packed a spiral notebook, pencils, a camera, and a magnifying glass.**

What is the CORRECT way to divide the word *spiral* into syllables?

Ⓐ sp • iral

Ⓑ spi • ral

Ⓒ spir • al

Ⓓ spira • l

8 Read this sentence from the passage.

> **I couldn't wait to explore the beach like a real marine biologist.**

Now complete the analogy below. Base your answer on what the word *real* means in the sentence above.

> ***Strong* is to *powerful* as *real* is to _____.**

Which word BEST completes the analogy?

Ⓕ adult

Ⓖ clever

Ⓗ curious

Ⓘ genuine

9 When Marina arrives at the beach, what is she eager to do?

Ⓐ smell the air

Ⓑ explore the beach

Ⓒ read her favorite book

Ⓓ build a large sandcastle

Name _____ Date _____

10 Read this sentence from the passage.

> **I found a tide pool with fish and other animals to inspect, so I
> pulled my book from my backpack and began flipping through
> the pages.**

What does the word *inspect* mean in the sentence above?

- Ⓕ not bother with
- Ⓖ look at carefully
- Ⓗ move to the side
- Ⓘ draw pictures of

11 How does Marina feel when she sees the boy jumping in the tide pool?

- Ⓐ confused
- Ⓑ jealous
- Ⓒ relieved
- Ⓓ upset

12 Read this sentence from the passage.

> **"The what?" he asked with a mixture of anger and confusion.**

Which word has the SAME sound as the underlined part of the
word *anger*?

- Ⓕ before
- Ⓖ declare
- Ⓗ frontier
- Ⓘ professor

13 Read this sentence from the passage.

"The shallow water in a tide pool is actually home to many tiny living creatures."

What does the word *shallow* mean in the sentence above?

Ⓐ not clean

Ⓑ not clear

Ⓒ not deep

Ⓓ not salty

14 Read this sentence from the passage.

The boy looked at his feet, shook his head, and mumbled, "Impossible."

What does the word *impossible* mean in the sentence above?

Ⓕ not possible

Ⓖ very possible

Ⓗ a little possible

Ⓘ with possibility

15 What can the reader tell from the passage?

Ⓐ Tide pools are not important.

Ⓑ Nothing can live in a tide pool.

Ⓒ Tide pools should be left alone.

Ⓓ Only fish can survive in a tide pool.

Name _____ Date _____

16 Which of the following shows that the boy will stop jumping in tide pools?

Ⓕ " 'What?' he demanded. 'I'm not hurting anything.' "

Ⓖ " 'The what?' he asked with a mixture of anger and confusion."

Ⓗ " 'Wow!' he exclaimed. 'There are things swimming in here.' "

Ⓘ " 'Wow, you know a lot about marine animals.' "

17 Read this sentence from the passage.

> **"That's because I want to be a marine biologist," I said**
> **with confidence.**

What does the word *confidence* mean in the sentence above?

Ⓐ ability to learn

Ⓑ ability to work

Ⓒ feeling of hope

Ⓓ feeling of certainty

18 What can the reader tell about Marina's mother?

Ⓕ She supports Marina's interests.

Ⓖ She spends little time with Marina.

Ⓗ She takes many vacations at the beach.

Ⓘ She is a scientist who studies the beach.

Read the article "How to Save Water" before answering Numbers 19 through 35.

How to Save Water

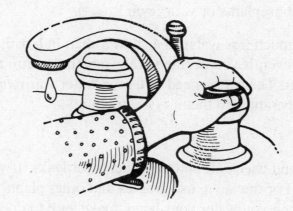

Have you ever been around when the water bill arrives at your house? Perhaps you've heard someone say, "Stop wasting water! The water bill is sky high!" Water costs a lot of money. Reducing the amount of water you use not only helps lower your family's water bill, it also helps the environment.

You might be wondering why water is so expensive. After all, water hardly seems scarce. It covers the majority of Earth, right? While that is true, most of Earth's water is in salty oceans. Because we cannot drink salt water, only a small amount of Earth's water is drinkable.

All living things need water to survive, so water is one of our most important natural resources. With a little effort, you can conserve water and also help keep down the water bill. You will be surprised at how easy it is to save water. Read the tips below to learn how.

Inside

From the time you wake up until you go to bed, pay attention to how much w
you use. How can you save water?

Do you wash your hands before you eat breakfast? If you do, turn off the w
while you lather the soap. Then, when you finish washing your hands, make su
you turn the faucet all the way off. Also remember to turn off the faucet when
put toothpaste on your toothbrush and while brushing your teeth. If your fau
when it is off, see if it can be fixed. If you have some trash to dispose of, do
in the toilet. Use a trash can instead.

Name _____ Date _____

Maybe you take a shower in the morning. Try to keep your time in the shower to less than ten minutes. Installing a low-flow showerhead, which reduces the amount of water you use, will help, too. Here is an interesting fact: If everyone in the United States shortened their showers by just a couple of minutes, it would conserve more than 80 billion gallons of water each year! If you let the water in the shower heat up before you get in, don't let it go down the drain. You can catch the water in buckets and use it to water houseplants or your lawn.

Usually you use much less water in a shower than in a bath. A shower is more refreshing, too. However, if you decide to take a bath, be sure to close the drain before you turn on the water. There's no need to let the water warm up first. Remember to adjust the water temperature so that it is not too hot.

Outside

Be an inspector and check all outdoor faucets for leaks. If you find a leaky faucet, fix it with a wrench. For the lawn, use grasses and other plants that need a minimal amount of water. When you water your lawn, make sure to do it either early in the morning or late in the evening. Watering during the hottest hours of the day increases evaporation. For example, if you water your lawn at 2:00 p.m., more than half of the water can evaporate. Watch where you are watering, too, and adjust any sprinklers that are watering your driveway or a sidewalk.

There are so many ways to save water. For fun, try to do at least one thing every day to conserve water. Do your community a favor and tell your friends some tips for conserving water, too. They will probably thank you. Every drop of water counts!

Name _____   Date _____

Now answer Numbers 19 through 35. Base your answers on the article "How to Save Water."

19 Read this sentence from the article.

> **Water costs a lot of money.**

Which word has the same sound as the underlined part of the word *money*?

- Ⓐ crumb
- Ⓑ dune
- Ⓒ phone
- Ⓓ stoop

20 Read this sentence from the article.

> **After all, water hardly seems scarce.**

What does the word *scarce* mean in the sentence above?

- Ⓕ costly
- Ⓖ invisible
- Ⓗ limited
- Ⓘ usable

21 Read this sentence from the article.

> **With a little effort, you can conserve water and also help keep down the water bill.**

What does the word *effort* mean in the sentence above?

- Ⓐ cause
- Ⓑ imagination
- Ⓒ patience
- Ⓓ work

Name _____ Date _____

22 Read this sentence from the article.

> **If you have some trash to dispose of, do not put it in the toilet.**

What does the word *dispose* mean in the sentence above?

- Ⓕ waste
- Ⓖ look for
- Ⓗ clean up
- Ⓘ get rid of

23 Read this sentence from the article.

> **Maybe you take a shower in the morning.**

What is the CORRECT way to divide the word *shower* into syllables?

- Ⓐ sh • ower
- Ⓑ show • er
- Ⓒ showe • r
- Ⓓ sho • wer

24 According to the article, what is one way that people can save water in the shower?

- Ⓕ by using a low-flow showerhead
- Ⓖ by adjusting the water temperature
- Ⓗ by closing the drain before turning on the water
- Ⓘ by turning off the water while lathering the soap

Name _____ Date _____

25 Which sentence from the article is an opinion?

Ⓐ "While that is true, most of Earth's water is in salty oceans."

Ⓑ "You will be surprised at how easy it is to save water."

Ⓒ "You can catch the water in buckets and use it to water houseplants or your lawn."

Ⓓ "Usually you use much less water in a shower than a bath."

26 Read this sentence from the article.

A shower is more refreshing, too.

What makes this statement an opinion?

Ⓕ The author wrote it.

Ⓖ It is the author's belief.

Ⓗ Most people agree with it.

Ⓘ It can be proven true or false.

27 Read this sentence from the article.

If you find a leaky faucet, fix it with a wrench.

Which letter is silent in the word *wrench*?

Ⓐ w

Ⓑ r

Ⓒ e

Ⓓ n

Name _____ Date _____

28 Read this sentence from the article.

> **Watering during the hottest hours of the day increases evaporation.**

Now complete the analogy below. Base your answer on what the word *increases* means in the sentence above.

> *Repairs* **is to** *breaks* **as** *increases* **is to** _____.

Which word BEST completes this analogy?

Ⓕ appears

Ⓖ grows

Ⓗ lowers

Ⓘ wastes

29 Read this sentence from the article.

> **Watch where you are watering, too, and adjust any sprinklers that are watering your driveway or a sidewalk.**

What does the word *sprinklers* mean in the sentence above?

Ⓐ things that leak water

Ⓑ things that save water

Ⓒ things that spray water

Ⓓ things that evaporate water

30 Read this sentence from the article.

> **Do your community a favor and tell your friends some tips for conserving water, too.**

What does the word *community* mean in the sentence above?

Ⓕ the opposite of your friends

Ⓖ a single person, not in a group

Ⓗ a group of people living together

Ⓘ the water source closest to your house

Name _____ Date _____

31 Read this sentence from the article.

Do your community a favor and tell your friends some tips for conserving water, too.

What does the word *favor* mean in the sentence above?

Ⓐ a list of tips

Ⓑ a secret to tell

Ⓒ an act of kindness

Ⓓ a command to follow

32 Read the chart below.

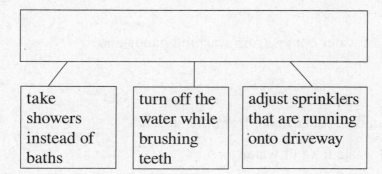

Which main idea BEST completes the chart?

Ⓕ where water comes from

Ⓖ ways to save water at home

Ⓗ why water costs a lot of money

Ⓘ how people waste water in the bathroom

33 What is the section *Outside* MOSTLY about?

Ⓐ the hottest part of the day

Ⓑ where to check for leaky faucets

Ⓒ how to use less water in the yard

Ⓓ the types of grasses and plants to use in a lawn

34 What can the reader conclude from this article?

Ⓕ People who take baths do not care about the environment.

Ⓖ Lawns and gardens should never be watered when the sky is dark.

Ⓗ If people could drink salt water, there would be less need to save water.

Ⓘ The biggest waste of water comes from washing hands and brushing teeth.

35 What generalization can the reader make from this article?

Ⓐ Leaky faucets can waste a lot of water.

Ⓑ Most people do not care about saving water.

Ⓒ There is much people can do to save water at home.

Ⓓ People usually leave the water on while brushing teeth.

Revising and Editing

Read the introduction and the passage "Mr. Ward's Lessons" before answering Numbers 1 through 7.

Evan wrote this passage about his teacher. Read his passage and think about the changes he should make.

Mr. Ward's Lessons

(1) Mine teacher, Mr. Ward, has always been interested in science and the

Arctic. (2) Last year, he traveled to the northern part of Alaska to study one of

the chilliest places on Earth. (3) This year, wev'e learned about the Arctic from

his stories and pictures. (4) In third grade, my teacher was Mrs. Vargas.

(5) Mr. Ward has shown us pictures of some of the animals he saw while

in Alaska. (6) My favorite pictures were of polear bears. (7) These huge bears

have features that help them survive in the extreme cold. (8) They have thicker fur than other bears. (9) Their feet work like oars to help them swim gracefuller, too. (10) A thick layer of blubber helps keep them warm and float in the icy water.

(11) We also learned about the walrus. (12) Mr. Ward told us that a bear might try to hunt a walrus. (13) A walrus can defend it with its long tusks. (14) A walrus also uses its tusks to climb onto the ice from the water. (15) A walrus is a huge animal. (16) An adult male walrus, called a bull, may weigh as much as one ton.

(17) Because of Mr. Ward's teaching, I hope to travel to one of the very colder places on Earth to study the animals that live there. (18) Then I can share my knowledge with others, too, just like Mr. Ward.

Now answer Numbers 1 through 7. Base your answers on the changes Evan should make.

1 What change should be made in sentence 1?

- Ⓐ change *Mine* to **My**
- Ⓑ delete the comma after *Ward*
- Ⓒ change *has* to **have**
- Ⓓ change *interested* to **interests**

Name _____ Date _____

2 What change should be made in sentence 3?

   Ⓕ change *This* to **These**

   Ⓖ change *wev'e* to **we've**

   Ⓗ change *stories* to **story's**

   Ⓘ change the period to a question mark

3 What change should be made in sentence 6?

   Ⓐ change *My* to **Me**

   Ⓑ change *favorite* to **most favoritest**

   Ⓒ change *polear* to **polar**

   Ⓓ change *bears* to **bares**

4 What change should be made in sentence 9?

   Ⓕ change *Their* to **There**

   Ⓖ change *feet* to **foots**

   Ⓗ change *swim* to **swam**

   Ⓘ change *gracefuller* to **more gracefully**

5 What change should be made in sentence 13?

   Ⓐ change *defend* to **defends**

   Ⓑ change *it* to **itself**

   Ⓒ change *its* to **it's**

   Ⓓ change *tusks* to **tusk's**

Name _____ Date _____

6 What change should be made in sentence 17?

(F) change *Ward's* to **Wards**

(G) delete the comma after *teaching*

(H) change *colder* to **coldest**

(I) change *live* to **lives**

7 Which sentence does NOT belong in this passage?

(A) sentence 4

(B) sentence 8

(C) sentence 14

(D) sentence 18

Read the introduction and the passage "No Fun" before answering Numbers 8 through 14.

Daisy wrote this passage about something that happened to her. Read her passage and think about the changes she should make.

No Fun

(1) My next-door neighbor, Alexa, broke her arm a few months ago.

(2) She got a cast, and I really liked it's bright orange color. (3) Everyone in class liked the cast, too, and they signed the cast to wish Alexa well.

(4) The cast was on her left arm and shes left-handed, so she was unable to write. (5) Since I sat next to her, I volunteered to write for her in class.

(6) From watching Alexa, it looked like having a broken arm had a lot of benefits. (7) I didn't realize it at the time, but I would soon learn how wrong my assumption was.

(8) Last week, I was riding my bike more faster than normal, and I fell. (9) I was wearing my helmet, of course, so I did not injure my head, but I did hurt my right wrist. (10) The doctor lined up the bones correctly and put a cast over my arm. (11) She said that while I wear the cast for six weeks, new bone cells will grow, and my bone will be as good as new.

(12) The next day at school, I asked everyone to sign my cast. (13) I tried to sign it my self, but it was much harder than I thought. (14) By lunch, my arm was itchy, and I couldn't scratch it. (15) It felt hot and sweaty, too. (16) So far, wearing the cast is no fun. (17) I'll definitely be

the most slowest bike rider on my block once the cast is off, and I'll be

careful about what I wish for!

_____

Now answer Numbers 8 through 14. Base your answers on the changes Daisy should make.

8 What change should be made in sentence 2?

- Ⓕ change *got* to **gets**
- Ⓖ change *I* to **me**
- Ⓗ change *it's* to **its**
- Ⓘ change *orange* to **oranje**

9 What is the BEST way to rewrite sentence 3?

- Ⓐ Everyone in class liked, signed, and wished the cast to wish Alexa well.
- Ⓑ Everyone in class liked the cast, too, and they signed it to wish Alexa well.
- Ⓒ It was liked, too, by everyone in class, and they signed it to wish Alexa well.
- Ⓓ In class everyone in it liked the cast and they signed the cast to wish Alexa well, too.

10 What change should be made in sentence 4?

- Ⓕ change *shes* to **she's**
- Ⓖ insert a period after *left-handed*
- Ⓗ change *unable* to **unabel**
- Ⓘ change *to* to **for**

Name _____ Date _____

11 What change should be made in sentence 8?

Ⓐ delete the comma after *Yesterday*

Ⓑ change *was* to **were**

Ⓒ delete the word *more*

Ⓓ change *fell* to **fallen**

12 Which sentence could BEST be added after sentence 9?

Ⓕ I always wear a helmet when I go skating, too.

Ⓖ My favorite color is green, so I got a green cast on my arm.

Ⓗ Unlike Alex, I am right-handed, so I write with my right hand.

Ⓘ At the hospital, an X-ray showed that the bone just above my wrist was broken.

13 What change should be made in sentence 13?

Ⓐ change *my self* to **myself**

Ⓑ change *but* to **until**

Ⓒ change *much harder* to **much more harder**

Ⓓ change *thought* to **thinking**

14 What change should be made in sentence 17?

Ⓕ change *definitely* to **definite**

Ⓖ delete *most* before *slowest*

Ⓗ change *once* to **one**

Ⓘ change *careful* to **carefull**

Read the introduction and the passage "A Simple Answer" before answering Numbers 15 through 19.

Malik wrote this passage about a family that enjoys a challenge. Read his passage and think about the changes he should make.

A Simple Answer

(1) Everyone in my family enjoys a challenging riddle. (2) In the mornings, we take turns writing a riddle for everyone else to solve.

(3) The one I wrote this morning took more long than usual to unravel.

(4) Here is what I wrote: What is the beginning of every end and the end of time and space?

(5) I watched my family as they carefully read the sentence. (6) There brows furrowed as they reread the question. (7) My father, usually the most creative, scratched his head. (8) My mother repeated the question over and over. (9) My brother and sister gave many answers, but they were all incorrect. (10) Finally, it was time to leave for work and school, and no one had identified the correct answer.

(11) That evening, my brother declared that hed given up trying to solve the puzzle, and my sister was convinced there was no correct solution.

(12) I offered to tell them, but they said they wanted to solve it theirself.

(13) However, they asked for a hint, so I suggested that everyone read it one last time and look at the words more closer. (14) My entire family thought even harder and made a final effort to solve the puzzle.

Name _____ Date _____

(15) Then a huge smile slowly grew across my sister's face and she

exclaimed, "I've got it! (16) The answer is the letter e! It's the beginning of the

words every and end. (17) It's also at the end of the words time and space!"

(18) My nodding head and knowing smirk told her that she had indeed

found the solution. (19) My sister was so proud of herself.

**Now answer Numbers 15 through 19. Base your answers on the changes
Malik should make.**

15 What change should be made in sentence 3?

Ⓐ change *The* to **That**

Ⓑ change *wrote* to **written**

Ⓒ change *more long* to **longer**

Ⓓ change *usual* to **usually**

16 What change should be made in sentence 6?

Ⓕ change *There* to **Their**

Ⓖ add a comma after *furrowed*

Ⓗ change *as* to **during**

Ⓘ change the period to a question mark

17 What change should be made in sentence 11?

Ⓐ delete the comma after *evening*

Ⓑ change *hed* to **he'd**

Ⓒ delete the comma after *puzzle*

Ⓓ change *correct* to **correctly**

Name _____ Date _____

18 What change should be made in sentence 12?

- Ⓕ change *offered* to **offer**
- Ⓖ change *but* to **since**
- Ⓗ change *solve* to **solving**
- Ⓘ change *theirself* to **themselves**

19 What change should be made in sentence 13?

- Ⓐ delete the comma after *However*
- Ⓑ change *so* to **as a result**
- Ⓒ insert a comma after *one*
- Ⓓ change *closer* to **closely**

Read the introduction and the article "Underwater Hockey" before answering Numbers 20 through 25.

So Yee wrote this article about a game she thought was interesting. Read her passage and think about the changes she should make.

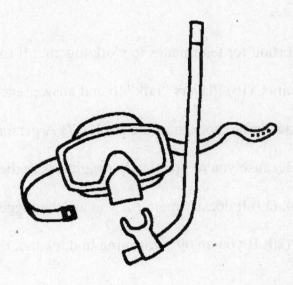

Underwater Hockey

(1) Do you like to swim? (2) Do you also like hockey? (3) If you said "yes" to these two questions, perhaps you're like the game "octopush."

(4) It's also known as underwater hockey. (5) A group of scuba divers in Britain invented the game in 1954. (6) Today the sport is becoming more popular. (7) It is offen played in places around the world.

(8) An underwater hockey game is played with two teams. (9) Each team has six players. (10) The game takes place at the bottom of a swimming pool. (11) Players wear flippers, a diving mask, a glove, a snorkel, and a cap to protect they're ears. (12) They use speciel sticks

about as long as a ruler to hit and slide a heavy puck along the bottom of the pool. (13) There is a goal at each end of the pool. (14) One team as in regular hockey tries to get the puck into the other team's goal and this is how you score.

(15) It is important for teammates to work together if they want to score many points. (16) Players "talk" to and answer each other by tapping their sticks on the bottom of the pool. (17) A person's size does not matter. (18) Because you're practically weightless in the water, everyone is equal. (19) It doesn't matter if you are the bigger person or the smallest person. (20) If you enjoy swimming underwater, this is a game you will love.

Now answer Numbers 20 through 25. Base your answers on the changes So Yee should make.

20 What change should be made in sentence 3?

    Ⓕ   change *said* to **saying**

    Ⓖ   change *these* to **this**

    Ⓗ   change *you're* to **you'd**

    Ⓘ   insert a comma after *game*

Name _____ Date _____

21 What change should be made in sentence 7?

   Ⓐ change *It is* to **Its**

   Ⓑ change *offen* to **often**

   Ⓒ change *world* to **World**

   Ⓓ change the period to a question mark

22 What change should be made in sentence 11?

   Ⓕ change *Players* to **Player**

   Ⓖ change *wear* to **wore**

   Ⓗ insert a comma after *cap*

   Ⓘ change *they're* to **their**

23 What change should be made in sentence 12?

   Ⓐ change *speciel* to **special**

   Ⓑ change *about* to **around**

   Ⓒ change *long* to **longer**

   Ⓓ change *of* to **on**

24 What is the BEST way to rewrite sentence 14?

   Ⓕ As in regular hockey, one team tries to score a goal by getting the puck into the other team's goal.

   Ⓖ One team in underwater hockey tries to get the puck, as in regular hockey, into the other team's goal to score a goal.

   Ⓗ As in regular hockey and in underwater hockey, one team tries to score a goal by getting the puck into the other team's goal.

   Ⓘ In regular hockey, one team tries to get the puck into the other team's goal to score and it is as this how you score in underwater hockey.

25 What change should be made in sentence 19?

    Ⓐ change *doesn't* to **don't**

    Ⓑ change *bigger* to **biggest**

    Ⓒ change *or* to **and**

    Ⓓ change *smallest* to **more smaller**

Name _____ Date _____

Writing Opinions

Read the poem "I'm nobody! Who are you?" before responding to the prompt.

I'm nobody! Who are you?
by Emily Dickinson

I'm nobody! Who are you?

Are you nobody, too?

Then there's a pair of us—don't tell!

They'd banish us, you know.

How dreary to be somebody!

How public, like a frog

To tell your name the livelong day

To an admiring bog!

Name _____ Date _____

Now respond to the prompt. Base your response on the poem "I'm nobody! Who are you?"

In "I'm nobody! Who are you?" the narrator would prefer to be a "nobody" rather than be the center of attention.

Think about whether or not you agree with the narrator.

Write a response that tells why or why not.

Use this space to make your notes before you begin writing. The writing on this page will NOT be scored.

_____

_____

_____

_____

_____

_____

_____

_____

_____

Name _____ Date _____

Begin writing your response here. The writing on this page and the next page WILL be scored.

_____

_____

_____

_____

_____

_____

_____

_____

_____

_____

_____

_____

_____

_____

_____

_____

Name _____ Date _____

_____

_____

_____

_____

_____

_____

_____

_____

_____

_____

_____

_____

_____

_____

Name _____ Date _____

Reading Complex Text

Read the play "Stay on the Trail!" As you read, stop and answer each question. Use evidence from the play to support your answers.

Stay on the Trail!

Cast of Characters:

Graciela, *a college student*

Raul, *a fourth grader and Graciela's cousin*

Holly, *Raul's friend and fourth-grade classmate*

Tessa, *Raul's friend and fourth-grade classmate*

Setting: *It is a sunny, Saturday afternoon. Graciela, Raul, Holly, and Tessa are hiking on a trail in the woods.*

Graciela: Another half-mile or so, and this trail will open into the wildflower field I was telling you about. My ecology class has been coming out here the last few Fridays to study some of the native plants.

Holly: The wildflowers are supposed to be in full bloom this week, aren't they Graciela?

Graciela: That's what my professor said. Either way, it should be a spectacular sight. And we couldn't have asked for better weather. Does anyone need some water? This trail is about to get very steep.

Raul: *(running ahead on the trail)* Hey, I have an idea! We can cut out some of our mileage if we just cut off the trail and climb the hill straight up. Follow me!

Raul begins leaves the trail and begins scrambling up the rocky slope. Holly and Tessa follow Raul, but Graciela hesitates.

1 How does the section *Cast of Characters* contribute to the reader's understanding of the play?

_____

_____

_____

Graciela: Actually, guys, we need to stay on the trail. I know that veering off the trail and climbing the slope would cut our distance in half, but you can do serious damage to the plants that way.

Holly, Tessa, and Raul pause, sending questioning glances at Graciela.

Tessa: Plants? But these just look like weeds. *(Wrinkling her nose, Tessa gestures at the vegetation covering the slope.)*

Graciela: *(laughing)* I know, I know–they're certainly not beautiful wildflowers; but they're still part of the natural vegetation and landscape. Foot traffic does more harm than you might think, wearing away the plants and the soil.

Raul: Like erosion? We're learning about erosion in science. *(He turns to Holly and Tessa.)* Remember how Mrs. Monese was telling us how the Grand Canyon was formed by erosion, as the river wore away the rock over millions of years? *(turning back to Graciela)* Is that the same thing?

Graciela: *(smiling)* Someone has been paying attention in science. It's the same concept, Raul. Erosion happens when the earth is worn away, whether by water, wind, gravity–or our feet! The plants' roots help hold the soil together.

2 According to Graciela, what is *erosion*?

_____

_____

_____

Name _____ Date _____

Holly: If we disturbed the plants and they couldn't grow, what would happen to the soil?

Graciela: Well, if there were a thunderstorm and heavy rain, the slope here in front of you would be in danger of washing away.

Tessa, Holly, and Raul look at each other wide-eyed. Then, all three kids retreat down the rocky slope, back to the trail. The group continues hiking until Raul stops in his tracks, frowns, and scratches his head.

Raul: Wait a second . . . I understand why we need to stay on the trail, but why didn't the people who built the trail just build it straight up the hill instead of a zig-zag pattern? *(panting)* We definitely would have reached the wildflower field by now!

Holly: I think they wanted to make sure we took the long, scenic route. Either that, or they wanted to make sure we got plenty of exercise! I think I'll take that drink of water now!

Laughing, Graciela hands Holly her water bottle.

Graciela: Believe it or not, the trail-builders were actually thinking about erosion when they made the trail zig-zag like that. Where the trail loops back and forth, that's called a "switchback." Think about it: if it rained, would the rain move down the hillside faster on a straight, steep trail or a gradual, zig-zag trail?

Tessa: Water would definitely move faster on the straight trail. It would be like riding the steep water coaster at the water park versus the lazy river float ride.

Holly: Hey, I don't mind this long, lazy-river approach for going up! If we had to climb straight up, I'd be way too tired to enjoy the wildflowers.

---

3   Why does Tessa compare the trail to a ride at the water park?

_____

_____

_____

Name _____ Date _____

Raul: *(looking at Graciela)* Are you sure our science teacher didn't hire you to trick us into a science lesson on the weekend?

Graciela: Ha, ha!

Raul: I'm just kidding, Graci. Seriously, though, most people who hike this trail probably don't know that they should stay on the trail and not take shortcuts. There should be signs posted, explaining why people should stay on the trail.

Holly and Tessa nod in agreement.

Graciela: Well, that sounds like a project for Mrs. Monese's science class. Maybe I could get my professor and some of my classmates to help out. *(winking)* See, Raul–it wasn't just a short lesson that Mrs. Monese hired me to teach; she was trying to trick you guys into organizing a big unit science project!

---

4 What is one lesson that Raul, Holly, and Tessa learn in this play? How does their experience on the trail help them learn this lesson?

_____

_____

_____

_____

_____

Name _____ Date _____

Justin and the Best Biscuits in the World

Answer Numbers 1 through 10. Base your answers on the novel *Justin and the Best Biscuits in the World*.

1 What is the setting at the beginning of Chapter 1?

Ⓐ a store

Ⓑ a playground

Ⓒ Justin's house

Ⓓ Anthony's house

2 Which word BEST describes Hadiya?

Ⓕ careless

Ⓖ fearful

Ⓗ neat

Ⓘ silly

3 How can the reader tell that Anthony is a kind person?

Ⓐ He sits on Justin's lumpy bed.

Ⓑ He helps Justin clean his room.

Ⓒ He tells Justin about his grandmother.

Ⓓ He plays basketball with Justin and Evelyn.

4 Which word BEST describes Grandpa?

- (F) brave
- (G) crabby
- (H) patient
- (I) rude

5 How does the author show that Justin and Grandpa have a special bond?

- (A) Justin and Grandpa laugh about the messy room.
- (B) Grandpa goes into Justin's room when he comes to visit.
- (C) Grandpa tells Justin about African American cowhands and the rodeo.
- (D) Justin sits on his bed and looks at Grandpa without moving.

6 Which of the following sentences helps the reader visualize how Justin looked when he went to Grandpa's ranch?

- (F) "Later that evening Justin packed his duffel bag."
- (G) "He was so excited about going with Grandpa he couldn't sleep."
- (H) "He polished his cowboy boots and shined his silver cowboy belt buckle."
- (I) "Justin lay in his bed imagining himself riding upon a horse under a dark starlit sky."

7 Which of the following sentences states an opinion?

- (A) Grandpa's ranch is quiet and tranquil.
- (B) Railroads link the country from East to West.
- (C) Black Lightning is the youngest of three horses.
- (D) Justin's great-great-grandfather rode cattle trails from Texas to Kansas.

8 What does Justin learn how to do in Chapter 5?

F make a bed

G catch fireflies

H cook biscuits and beans

I ride a horse without a saddle

9 In Chapter 7, what lesson does Grandpa teach Justin?

A Housework is for women.

B The better you do a job, the easier it becomes.

C Bill Picket was the greatest cowhand that ever lived.

D Only men can learn how to take care of horses and cattle.

10 Why does Justin MOST LIKELY want to bake biscuits for his family?

F to make Evelyn mad at him

G to share a treat with his best friend Anthony

H to show that he was a better cook than Hadiya

I to show how much he had changed while visiting Grandpa

Phineas L. MacGuire . . . Gets Slimed!

Answer Numbers 1 through 10. Base your answers on the novel *Phineas L. MacGuire . . . Gets Slimed!*

1 What is Mac's goal at the beginning of the novel?

Ⓐ to make a volcano

Ⓑ to be called Listerman

Ⓒ to teach Sparky how to talk

Ⓓ to be the best fourth-grade scientist

2 How does the reader know that Mac does not live close to his school?

Ⓕ He changes his goals.

Ⓖ He dreams of being a superhero.

Ⓗ He rides the bus to get to his house.

Ⓘ He is dragging his backpack down the street.

3 Which word BEST describes Mac in Chapter 2?

Ⓐ gloomy

Ⓑ messy

Ⓒ stern

Ⓓ uneasy

Name _____ Date _____

4 Why does Sarah clean the refrigerator?

   Ⓕ   Mac made a mess in it.

   Ⓖ   Margaret spilled juice in it.

   Ⓗ   Mac's mom offered to pay her extra.

   Ⓘ   She was looking for something to feed Margaret.

5 Which event happens FIRST in Chapter 4?

   Ⓐ   Mac changes his goals.

   Ⓑ   Ben raises his hand to run for class president.

   Ⓒ   Mac and Aretha talk on the jungle gym at recess.

   Ⓓ   Mrs. Tuttle blows the whistle to tell the students to come inside.

6 In Chapter 5, which event shows that Mac has BOTH good and bad things happen in his life?

   Ⓕ   His best friend moves away, but Aretha becomes his new best friend.

   Ⓖ   He gets the teacher he wants, but he gets the babysitter he does not want.

   Ⓗ   He has to write a book report, but he is able to write it about a book he has already read.

   Ⓘ   His mom and stepdad are going away for the weekend, but his dad is going to take care of him.

7 What happens when Ben asks Mac to be his vice president?

   Ⓐ   Mac laughs at Ben.

   Ⓑ   Mac turns Ben down.

   Ⓒ   Mac thinks it is a great idea.

   Ⓓ   Mac draws a poster for their campaign.

8 What does Ben do to get Aretha to be his vice president?

    Ⓕ   He starts to tell jokes.

    Ⓖ   He pays her some money.

    Ⓗ   He tells her a bunch of lies.

    Ⓘ   He promises to do her chores.

9 Which conclusion can the reader draw about Mac based on information in Chapter 13?

    Ⓐ   Mac has moved several times.

    Ⓑ   Mac thinks Ben is the smartest kid he knows.

    Ⓒ   Mac keeps his desk clean so he can do experiments.

    Ⓓ   Mac always checks in with Sarah as soon as he gets home.

10 Why does Ben's dad fly in from Seattle?

    Ⓕ   Ben is elected president.

    Ⓖ   Ben is elected vice president.

    Ⓗ   Ben builds a mold museum for Mac.

    Ⓘ   Ben wins first place in the science fair.

Name _____ Date _____

Sea Turtles: Ocean Nomads

Answer Numbers 1 through 10. Base your answers on the book *Sea Turtles: Ocean Nomads*.

1 What setting is described at the beginning of this book?

Ⓐ a desert

Ⓑ a grassy plain

Ⓒ a tropical island

Ⓓ a snow-capped mountain

2 What is the topic of this book?

Ⓕ parrot fish

Ⓖ sea turtles

Ⓗ rain forests

Ⓘ coral caves

3 Why do parrot fish have teeth that are fused together?

Ⓐ to eat shellfish

Ⓑ to hold on to sea plants

Ⓒ to grind up chunks of coral

Ⓓ to crush the bones of sea turtles

Name _____ Date _____

4 How are humans and sea turtles ALIKE?

- Ⓕ They breathe air.
- Ⓖ They have a hard shell.
- Ⓗ They usually live on land.
- Ⓘ They are types of reptiles.

5 Why is tar a problem for sea turtles?

- Ⓐ It makes it difficult for them to breathe.
- Ⓑ It makes it harder for them to stay afloat.
- Ⓒ It covers their eyes, nose, and mouth.
- Ⓓ It softens their shell, flippers, and beak.

6 Which animal is most like a sea turtle?

- Ⓕ fish
- Ⓖ bird
- Ⓗ horse
- Ⓘ snake

7 What do scientists want to learn from their experiment with Myrtle?

- Ⓐ how turtles eat
- Ⓑ how turtles see
- Ⓒ how turtles hear
- Ⓓ how turtles breathe

8　Which of the following is a source of noise pollution that could affect sea turtles?

　　Ⓕ　ship engines

　　Ⓖ　whales singing

　　Ⓗ　people's voices

　　Ⓘ　waves crashing

9　Why are the FIRST few days of a sea turtle's life the most dangerous?

　　Ⓐ　It has to look for its mother in the sea.

　　Ⓑ　It has to find food as soon as it hatches.

　　Ⓒ　It has to cross the beach to get to the ocean.

　　Ⓓ　It has to dig out of the sand without being able to see.

10　Which conclusion can the reader draw from this book?

　　Ⓕ　Water pollution never affects sea turtles.

　　Ⓖ　Soon there will not be any sea turtles left.

　　Ⓗ　Many people are trying to help sea turtles.

　　Ⓘ　Sea turtles should only live in marine parks.